THiS BooK BeLoNGS To

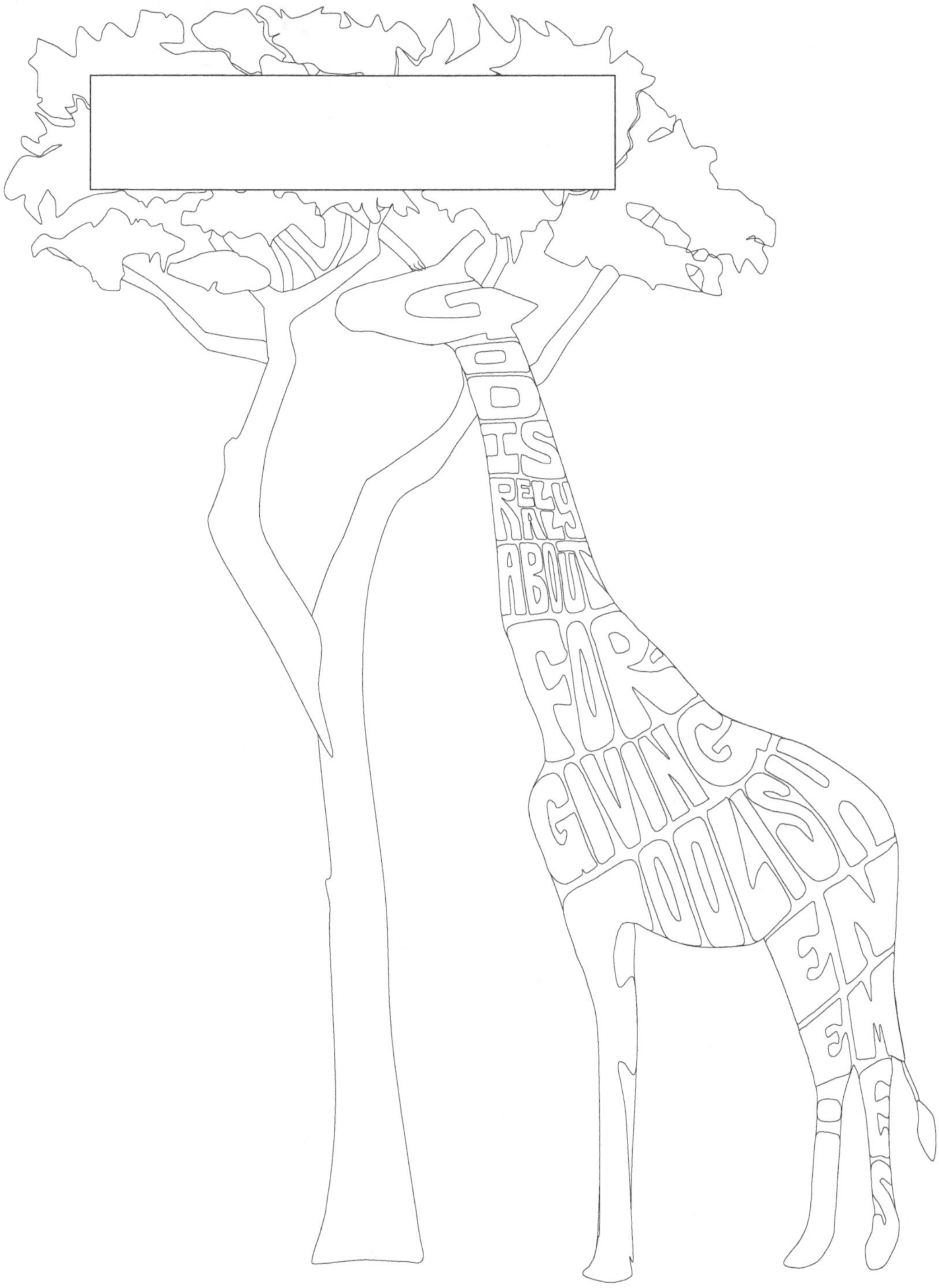

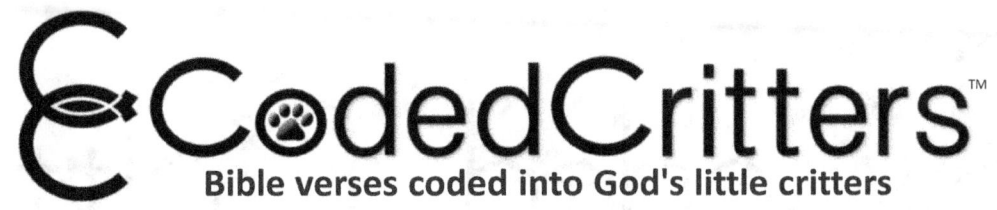

CodedCritters™

Bible verses coded into God's little critters

The name of the Critter is the acronym of the paraphrased Bible verse.

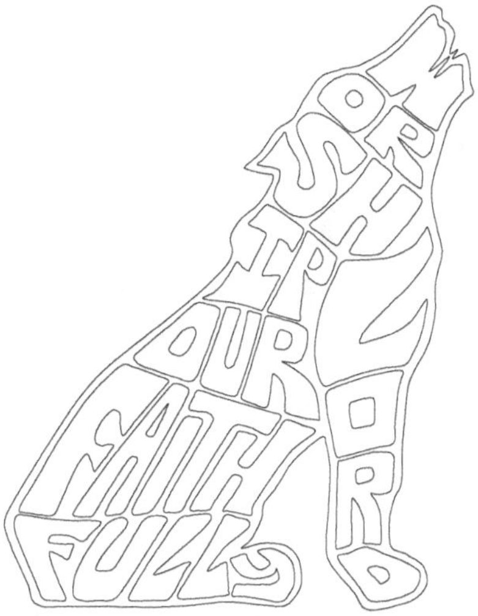

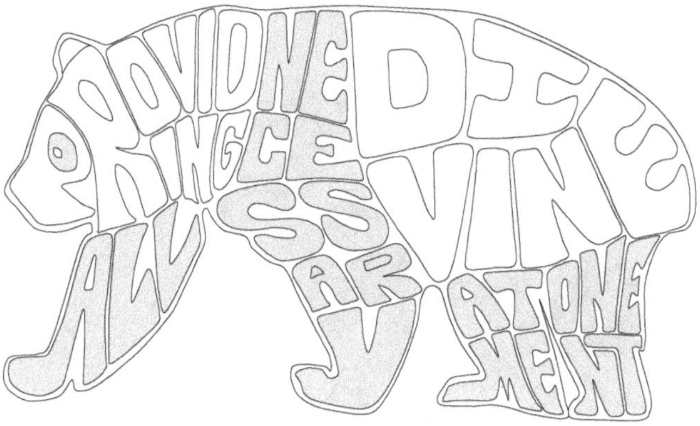

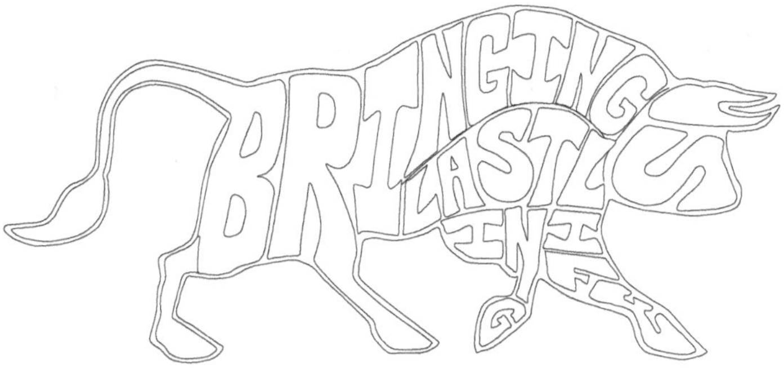

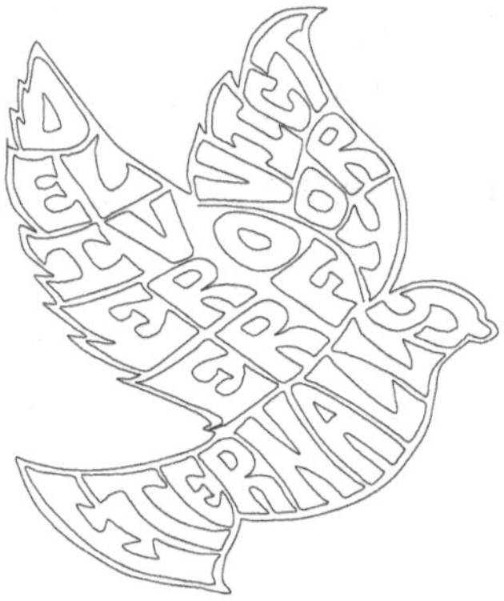

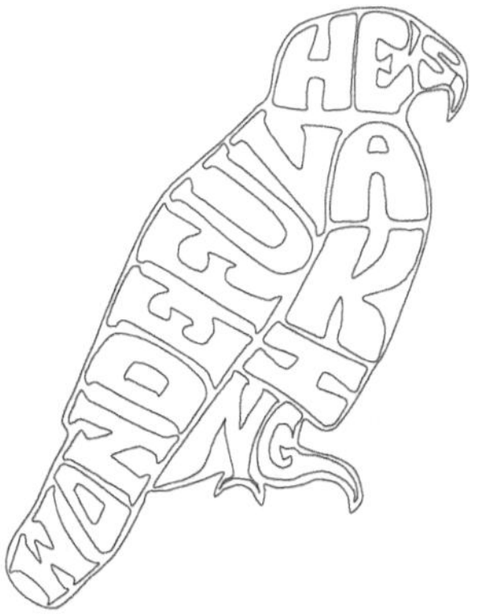

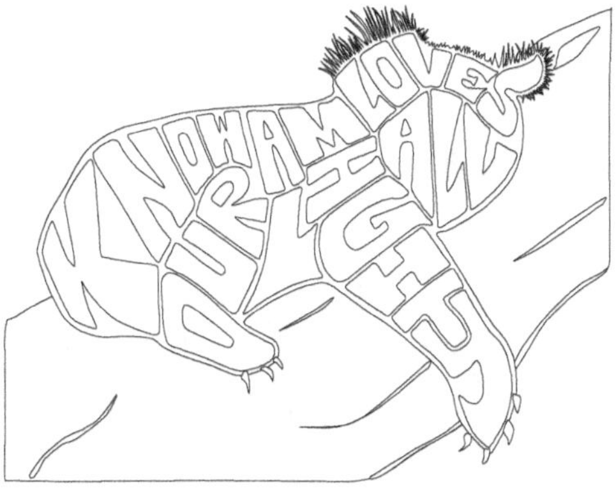

Coded Critters Creator & Artist: Michael Massanelli

www.CodedCritters.com

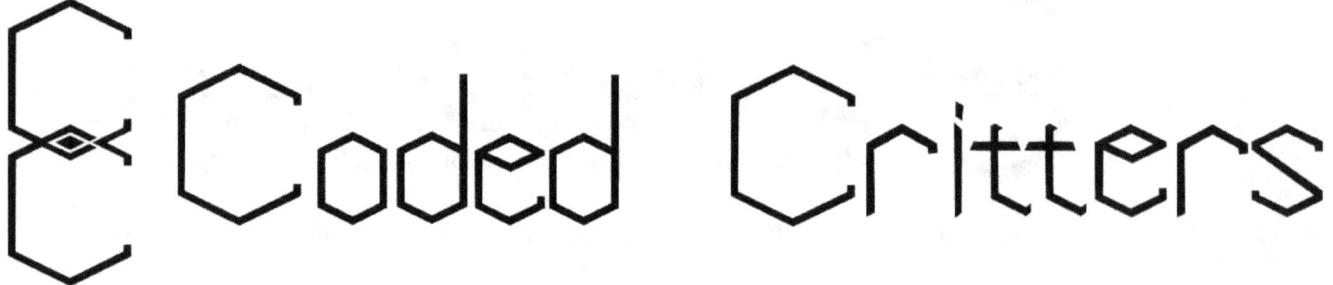

Coded Critters

But ask now the Critters, and they shall teach thee; and the birds of the air,
and they shall tell thee, and the fishes of the sea shall declare unto thee…
In whose hand is the soul of every living thing, and the breath of all mankind.
-Job 12 7-10

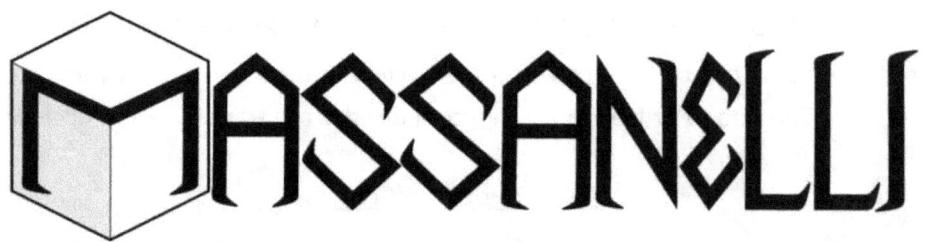

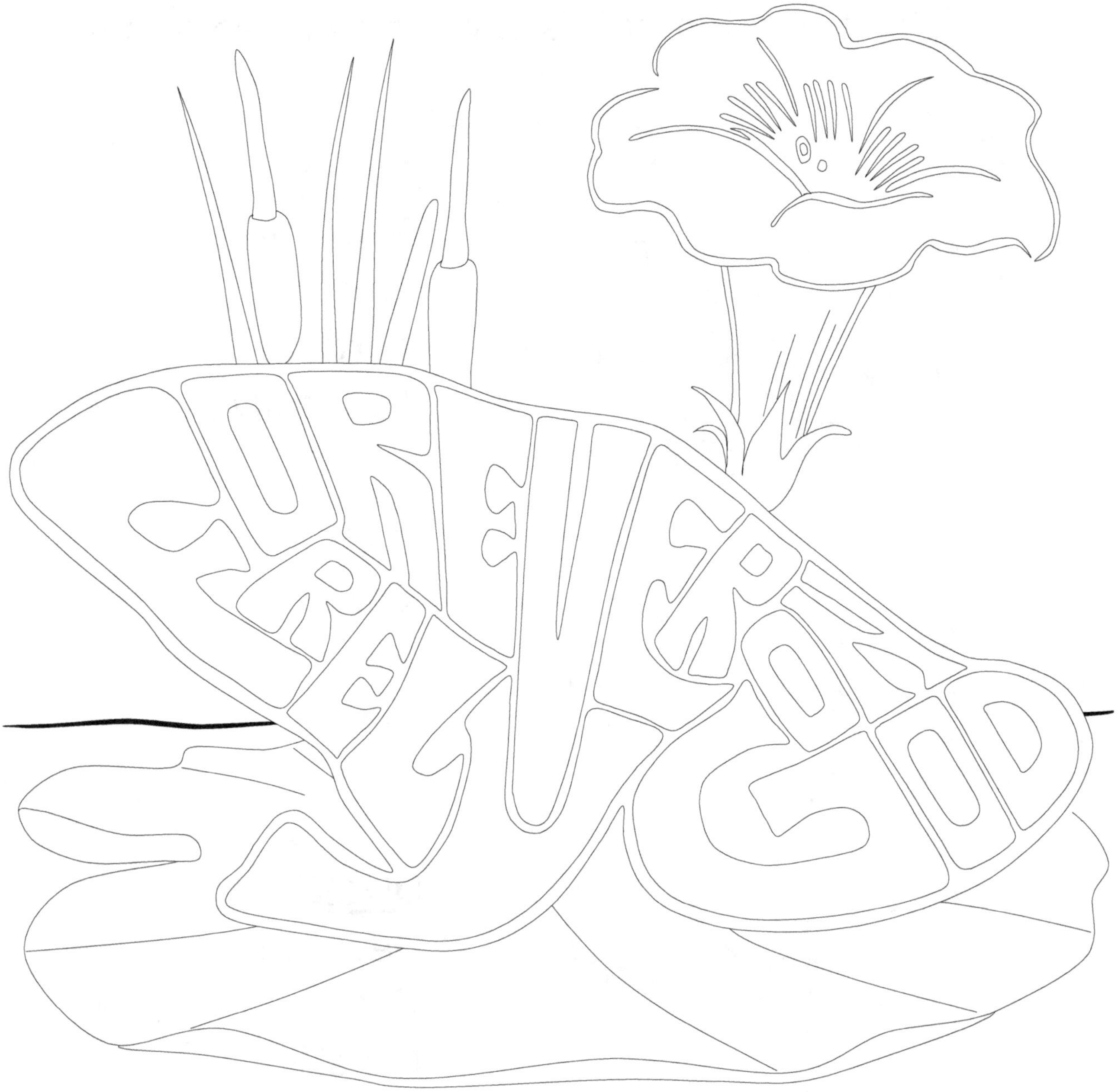

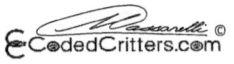

Proverbs 3:5

ACRONYM: An abbreviation formed from the initial letters of other words and pronounced as a word.

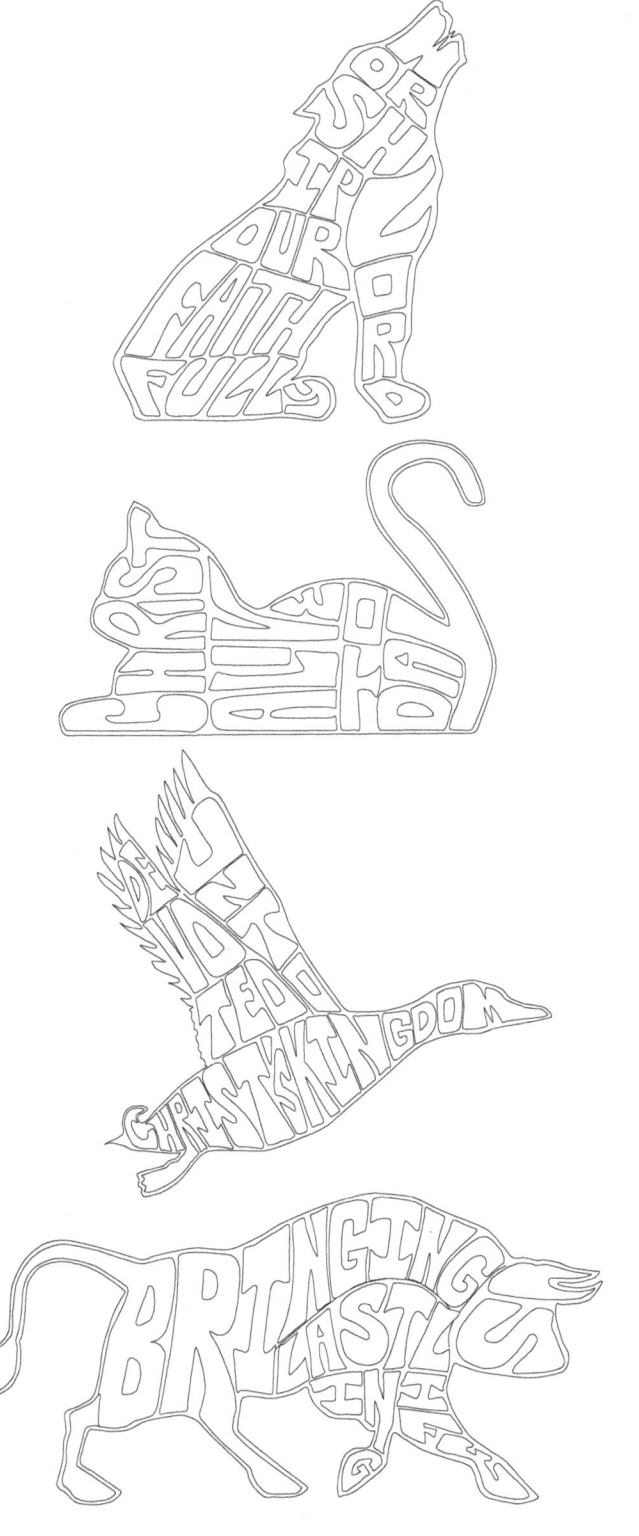

WOLF
Worship
Our
Lord
Faithfully

CAT
Christ
Alive
Today

DUCK
Devoted
Unto
Christ's
Kingdom

BULL
Bringing
Us
Lasting
Life

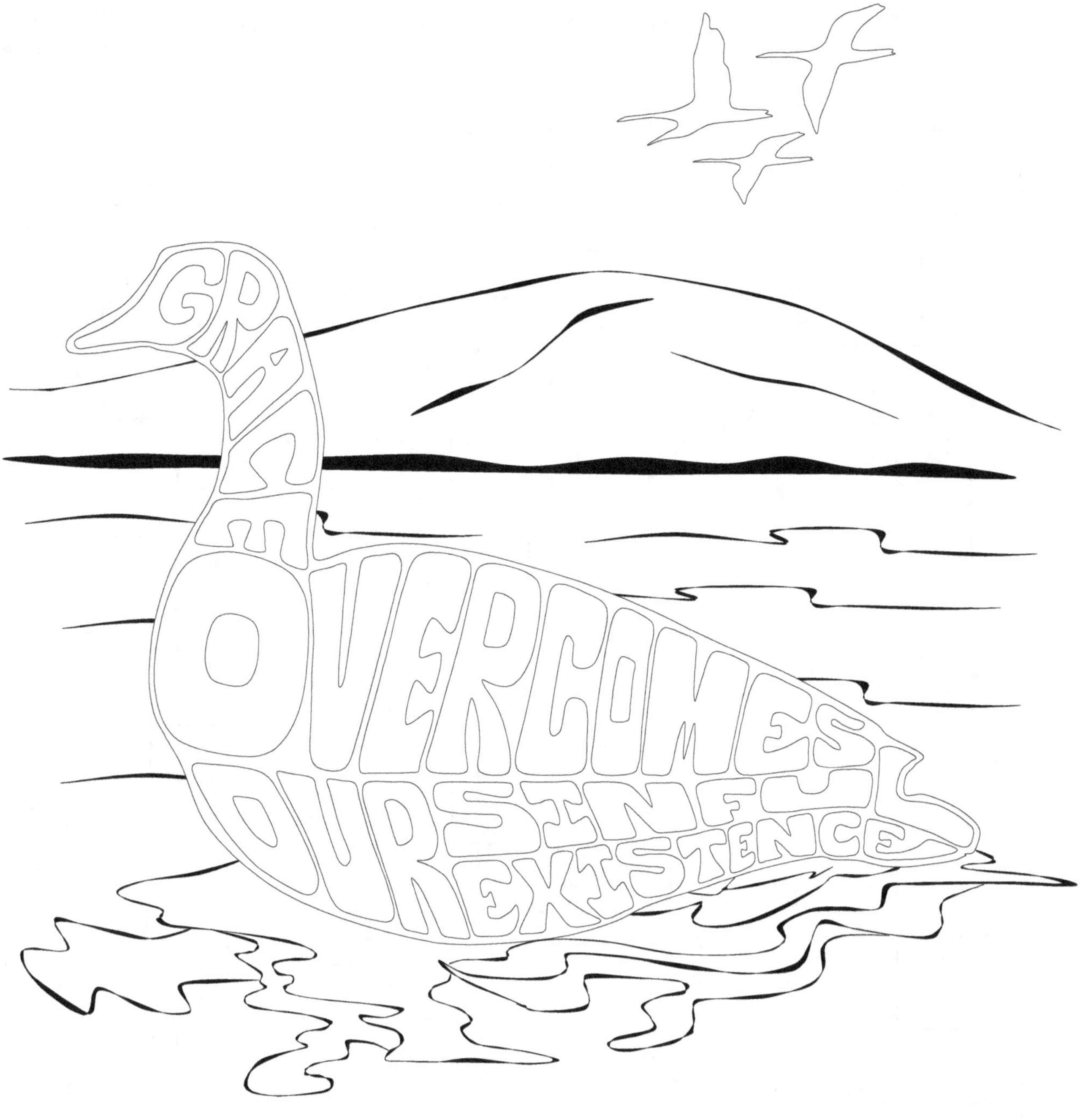

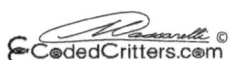

Romans 6:14

GRACE OVERCOMES OUR SINFUL EXISTENCE

A MAZE IN GRACE

Follow Jesus down the narrow path of righteousness.
There are many paths that seem right but only one is The Way.

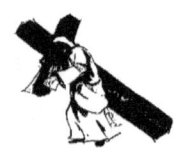

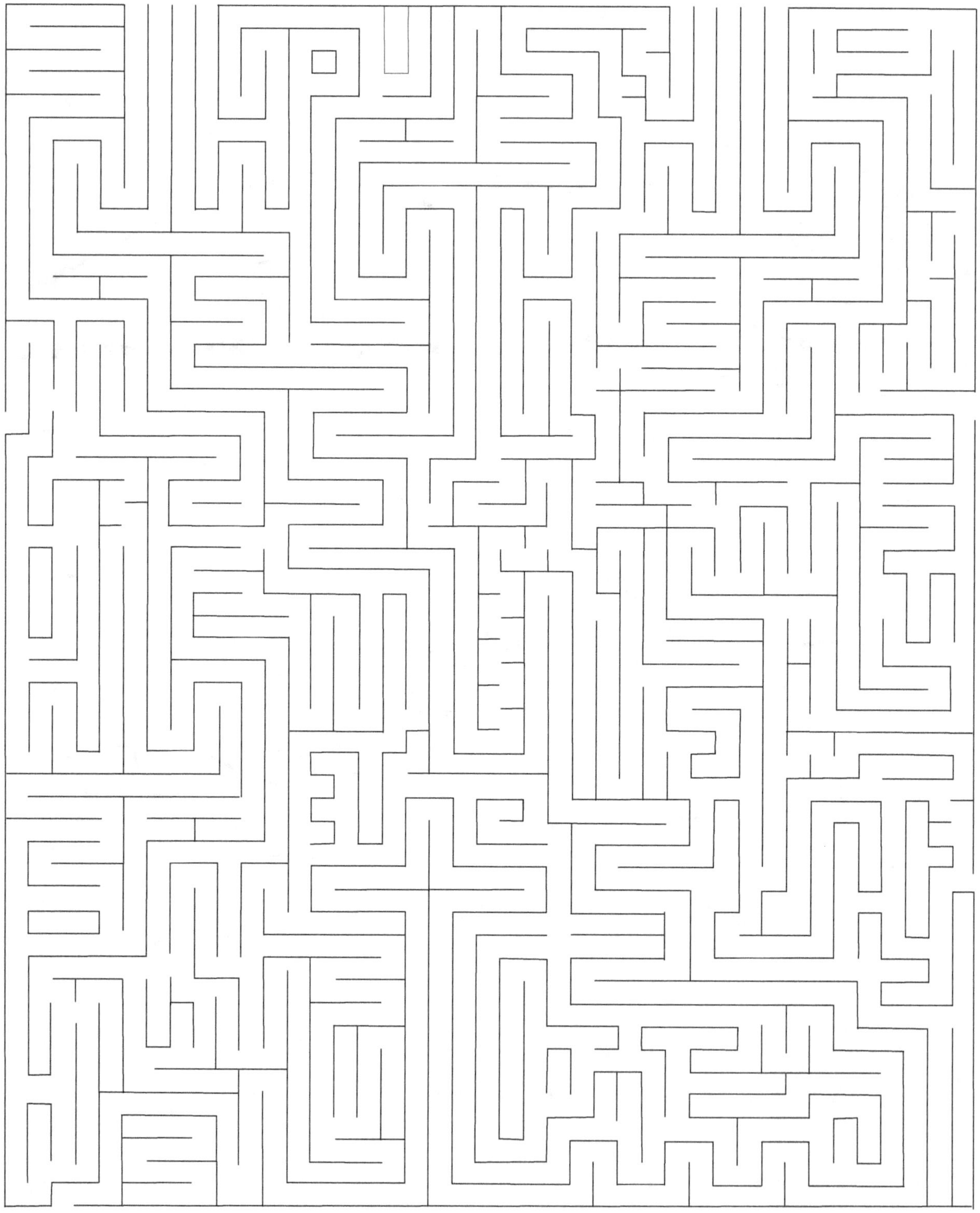

Heaven

NEW TESTAMENT

Acts   Galatians   Luke   Philemon   Thessalonians
Colossians   Hebrews   Mark   Philippians   Timothy
Corinthians   James   Matthew   Revelation   Titus
Ephesians   John   Peter   Romans   ...who's missing?

```
C P C E Y L E A E I O I L O I M J R I N J U
T E A J O O V R R S N T U S N M A E F N E G
W N S I P U O E V S U J Y L I C E C T N V T
B E E A R S Y S O L S E Y H T O M I T T M B
D F F G S L T W H G H O B S T L F L A I M K
W E S E M A J J A M S E O S F O T C R T A M
W F E L E C O R I N T H I A N S L E D U J O
J S V E N T H R A C L M J C N S I V E S G S
D T U O F S N I R E V E L A T I O N D N N T
O L R N I N T K K O E M I N O A E R D A V D
I V E W S A O O U B M A T G L N P E I E H G
E J E T L G R M C E L A I T A S T N P O P H
I U E A I D T A H A U O N S A L O O H I H S
C E G B R E H E S A K M G S L L A D I K I A
R T U U S O N S R W E A T Y A I Y N L R L W
A P R E S O E G R G E N R S E E L O I M E T
H A R T T H M E O I A R S E S A P W P J M I
H W E H T T A M I N P E B M R E T E P M O M
G D E O N F R W D G H R C E P H E S I A N S
U I S T E S K E D T A F E T H L U E A G R E
T M H A M A A N L I D E R I E R C M N W T A
B I C E L S S E L C O D C T T S K Y S I F E
```

SHAPE FINDER
How many Squares ☐ can you find in the puzzle?

A. 20   C. 40   E. 50

B. 10   D. 30   F. Other

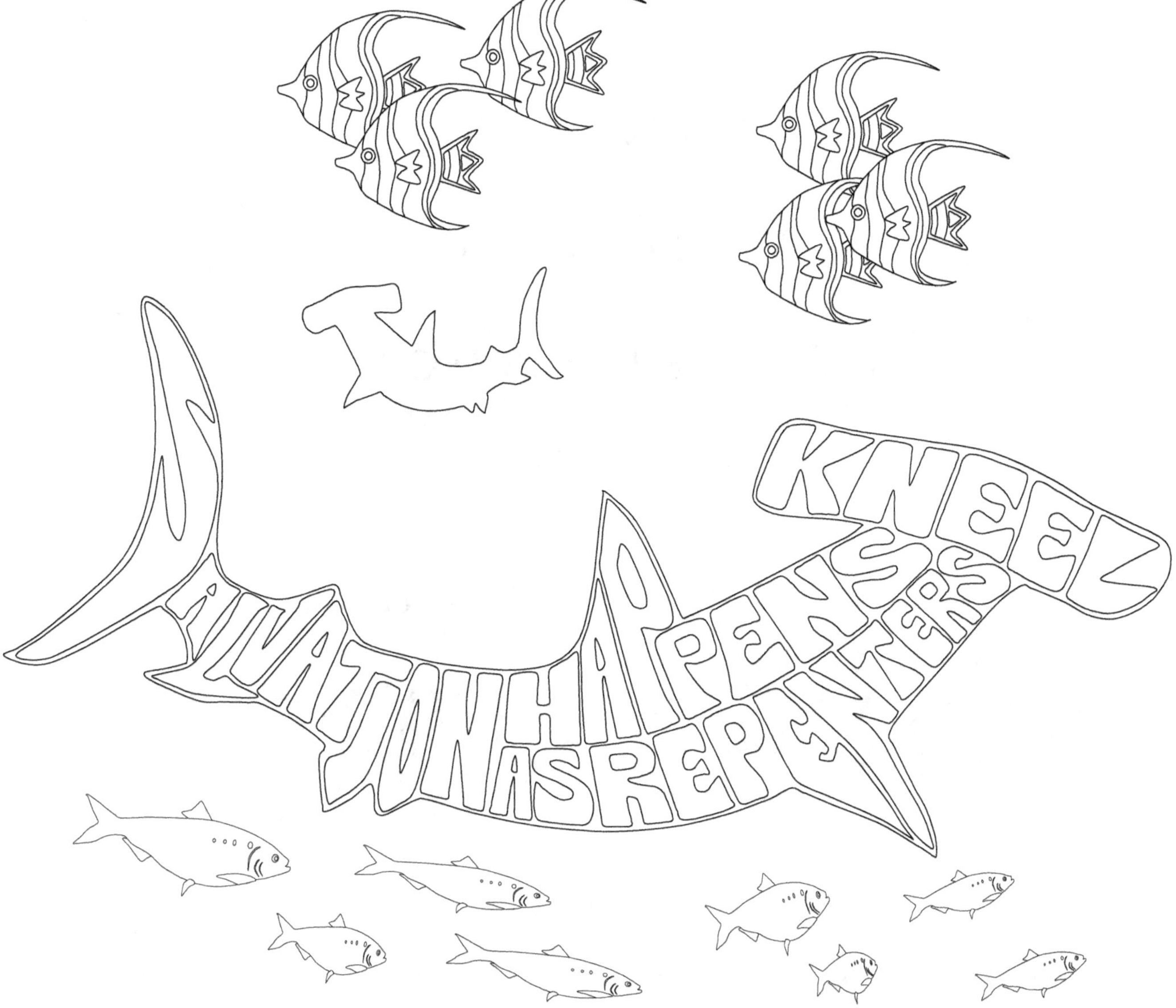

Matthew 4:17

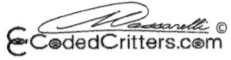

ANAGRAM: A word or phrase formed by rearranging
the letters of another, such as *PRAISE* can also spell *ASPIRE.*

OWL = LOW

HORSE = SHORE

LADYBUG = BALD GUY

ELEPHANT = THE PLANE

DOLPHIN = PIN HOLD

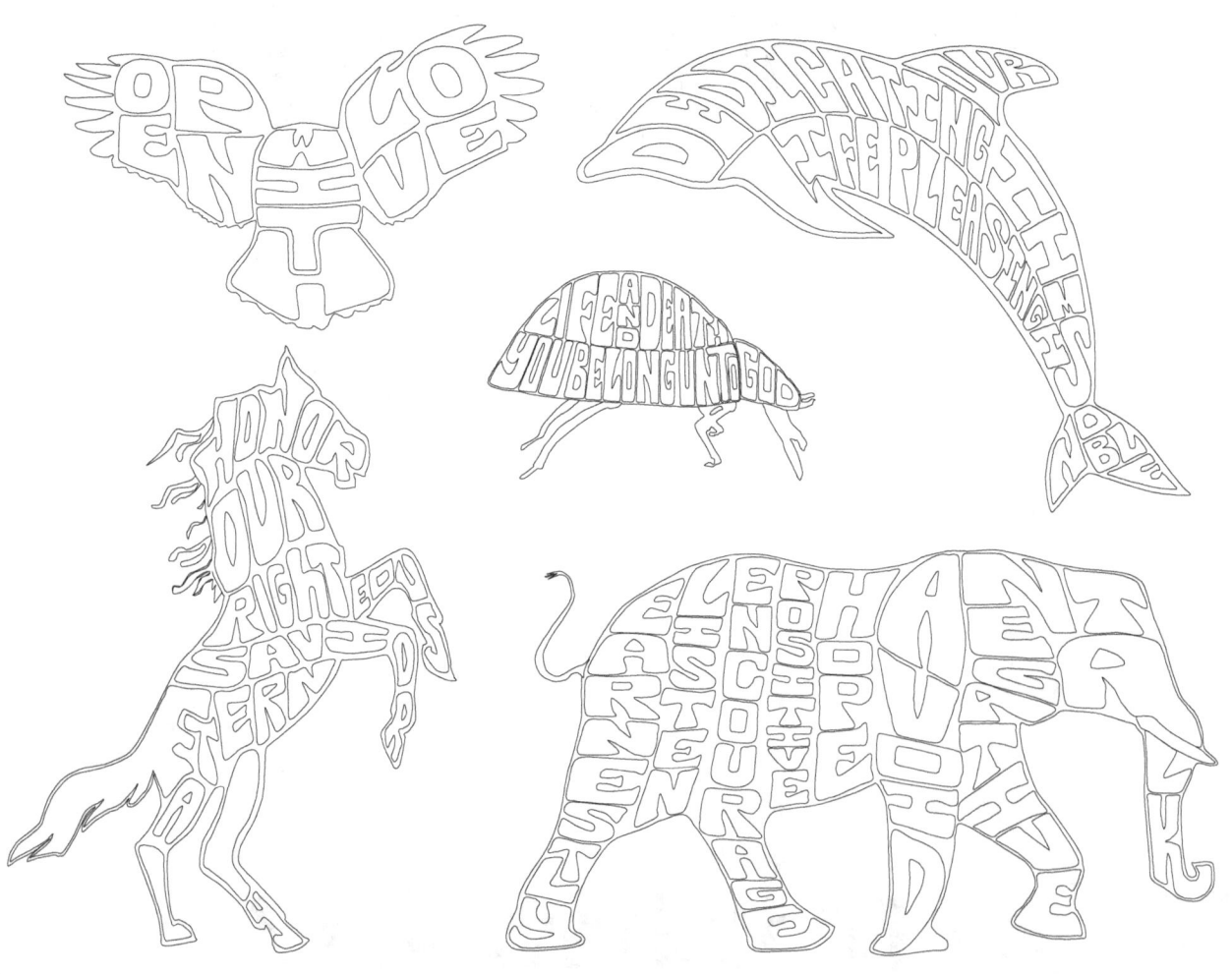

DOT TO DOT

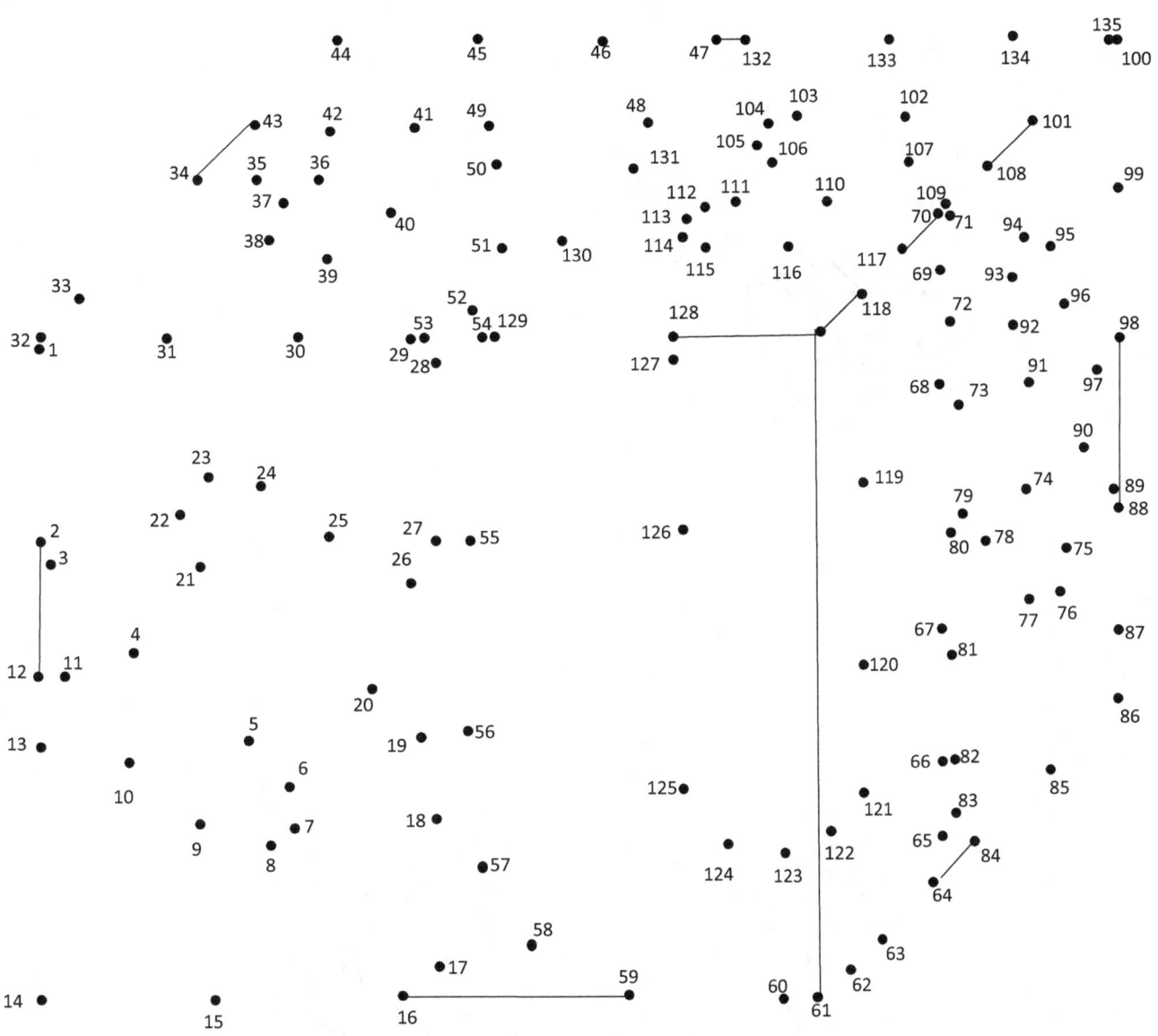

Verses to the image above:

Ephesians 2:20   Matthew 21:42   1 Peter 2:6   Acts 4:11   1 Peter 2:7

9

TIC TAC TOE

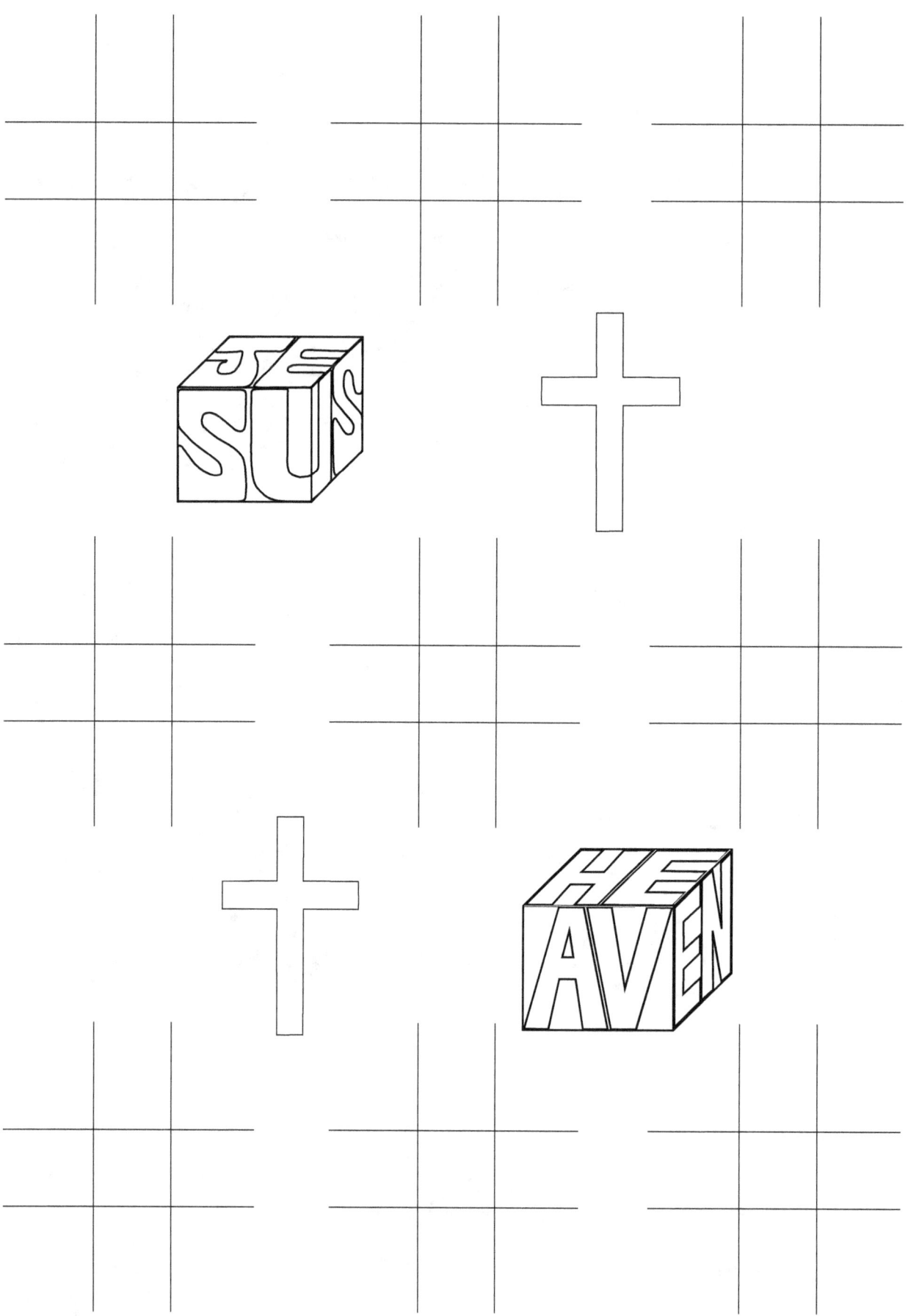

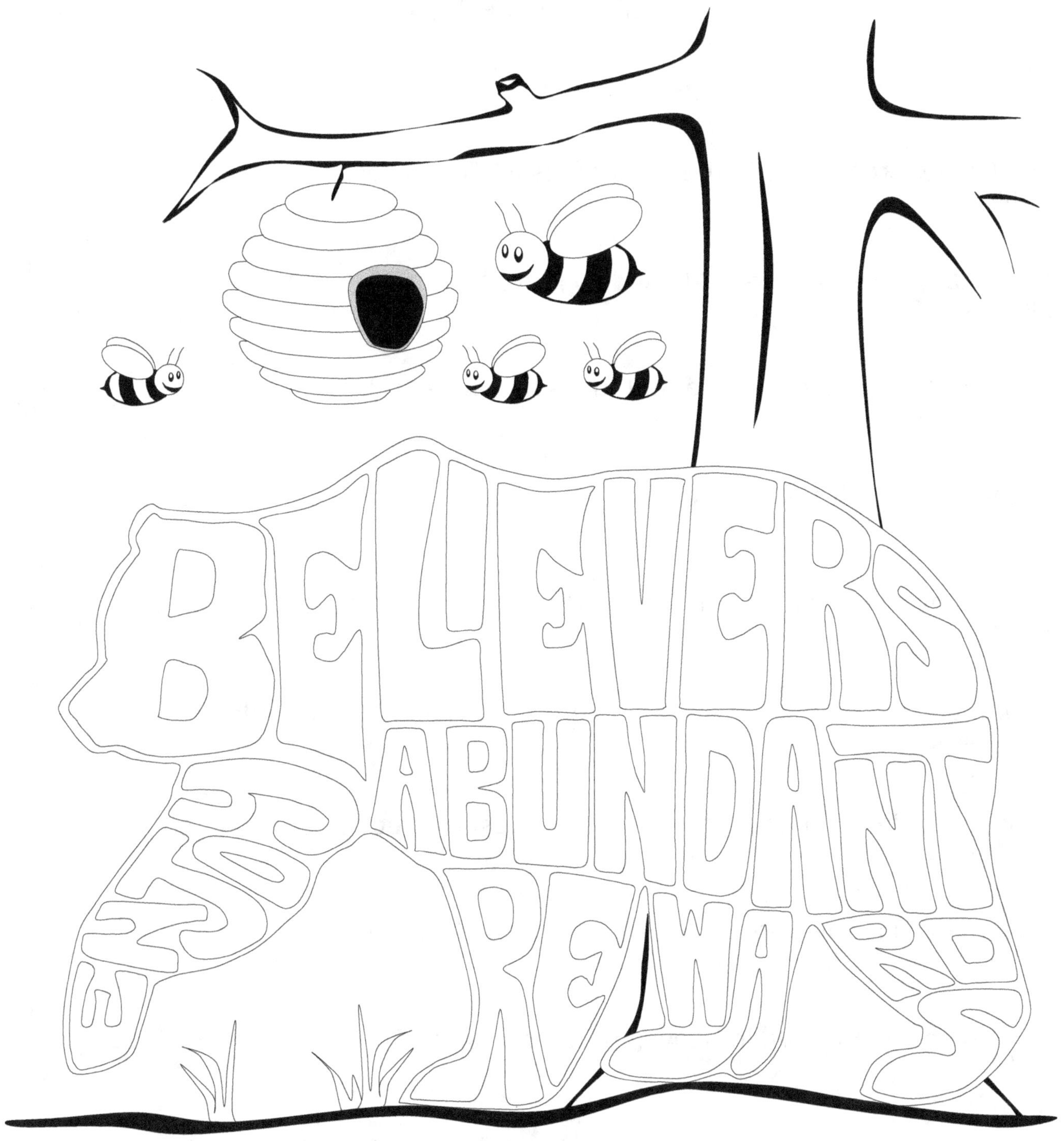

John 10:10

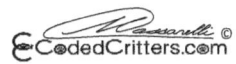

BIBL3 TRiViA

How many Crosses are in the story of Jesus' Crucifixion?_____
Matthew 27:38

How many times was Jesus denied by Peter?_____
Matthew 26:75

For how many pieces of silver did Judas betray Jesus?_____
Matthew 26:15

0

What hour was Jesus crucified?_____
Mark 15:25

How many days was Jesus in the heart of the Earth?_____
Matthew 12:40

How many days did Jesus say it would take to rebuild the temple?_____
John 2:19

How many days did it take for Jesus to be resurrected?_____
1 Corinthians 15:4

How many days did Joseph and Mary look for Jesus in Jerusalem? _____
Luke 2:46

How many bear record in Heaven that Jesus is the Christ born of God?_____
1 John 5:7

How many hours of darkness were there at the Crucifixion?_____
Matthew 27:45

It's believed that Jesus was how old when He was Crucified?_____
Luke 3:23 + 3 Passovers of John 2:13, 6:4, and 11:55

Unscramble the Critter's name then match it to the verse that fits it best by drawing a line from the name, to the Critter, and then to the proper verse.

ALES

A Life Lived In Gratitude
Always Takes Over Resentment

Revelation 1:18

_____

AIGLALORT

Deuteronomy 4:29

_____

Sin Keeps Us Needing Kindness

ACT

Isaiah 59:2

_____

Seek Eternal Abiding Love

NKUKS

Psalms 118:24

_____

Christ Alive Today

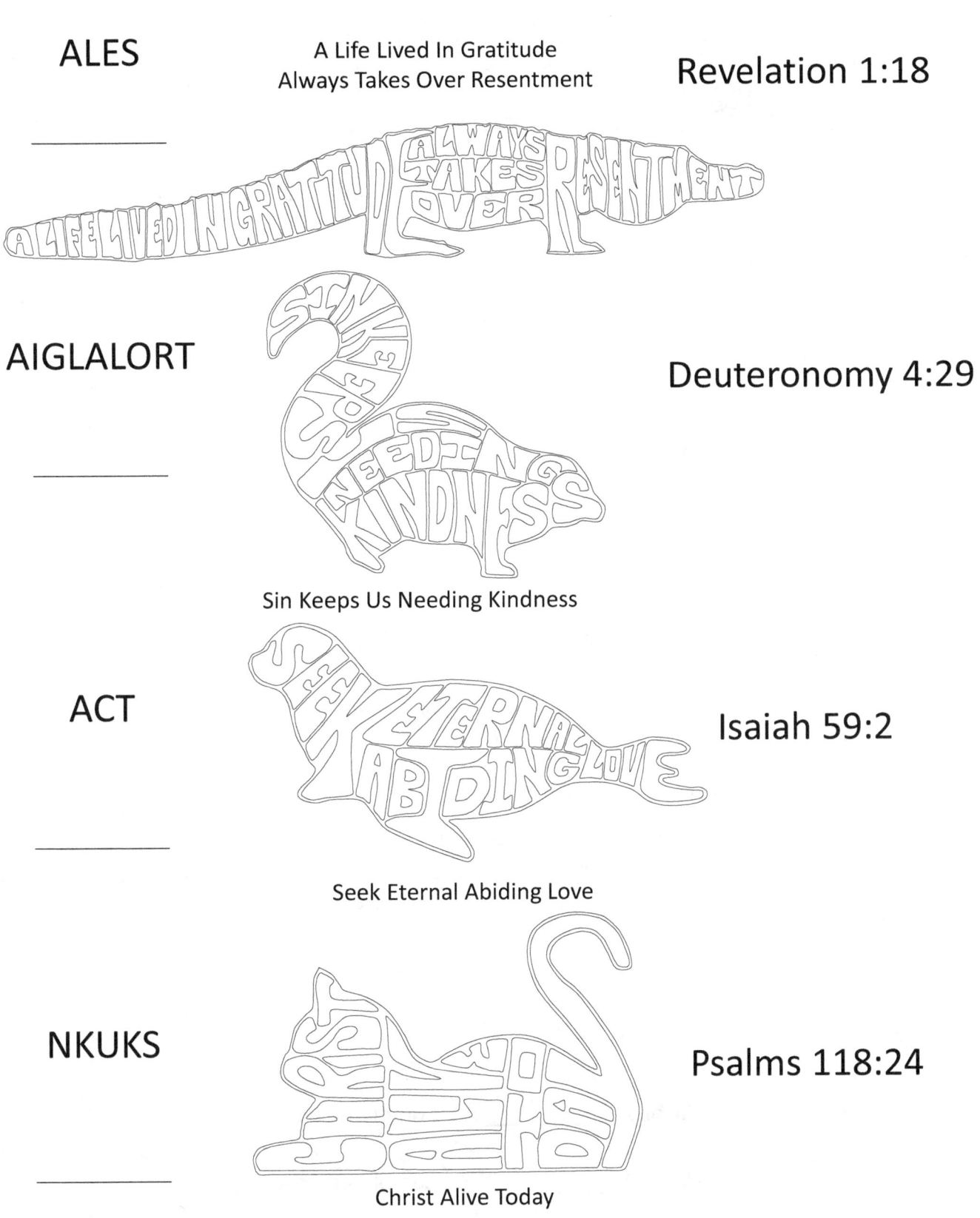

13

CODED CUBES

Take turns connecting the dots with a single straight line up and down or left to right. When the connected lines complete a box, color that box with your color. When all the dots are connected and all the completed boxes are colored count the colored boxes to see who has more.

Player #1	x	Player #2

Player 1 _____ Completed Boxes _____

Player 2 _____ Cumpleted Boxes _____

14

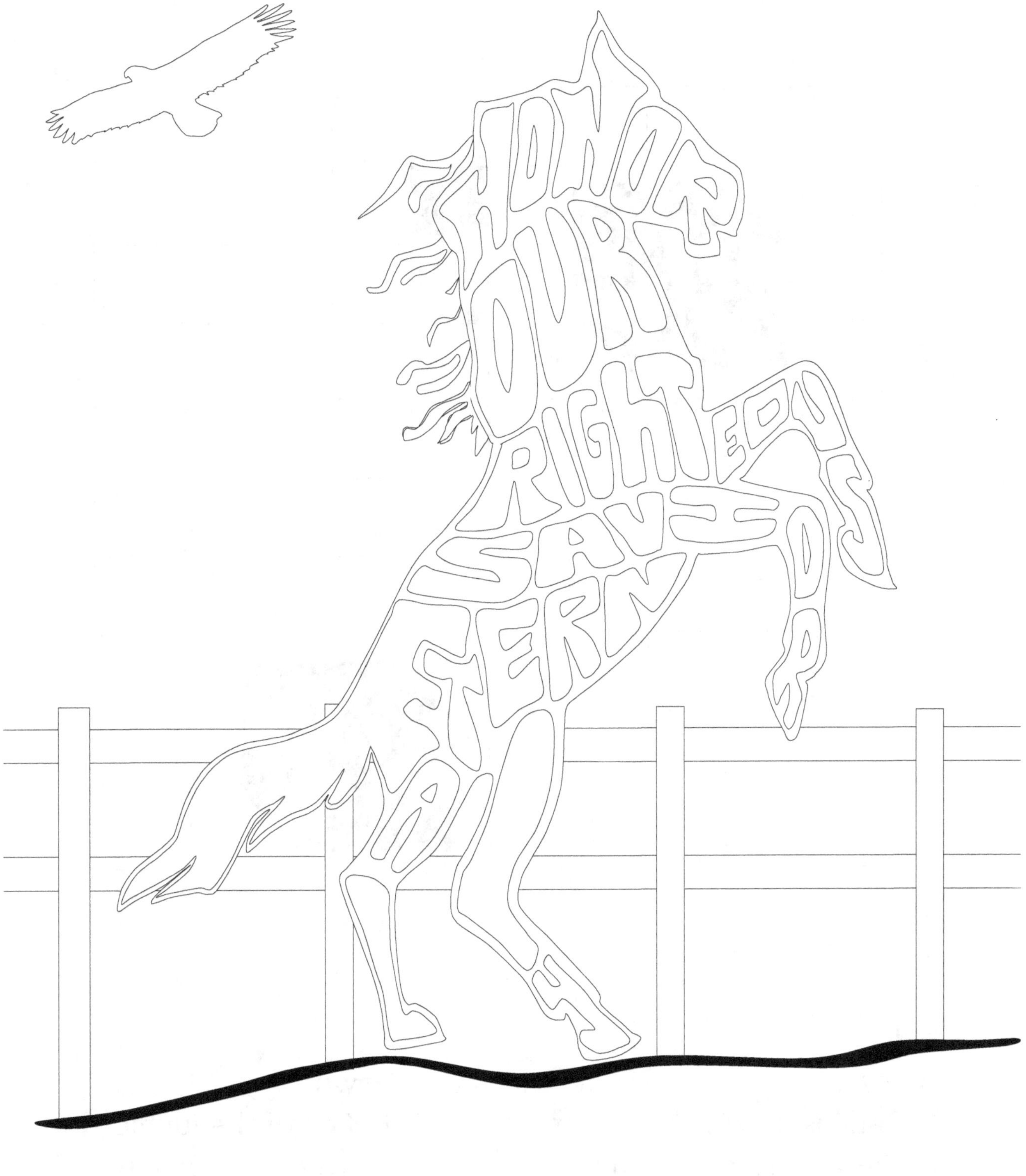

1 Samuel 2:30

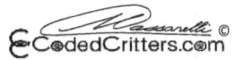

CRITTER CROSSWORD PUZZLE

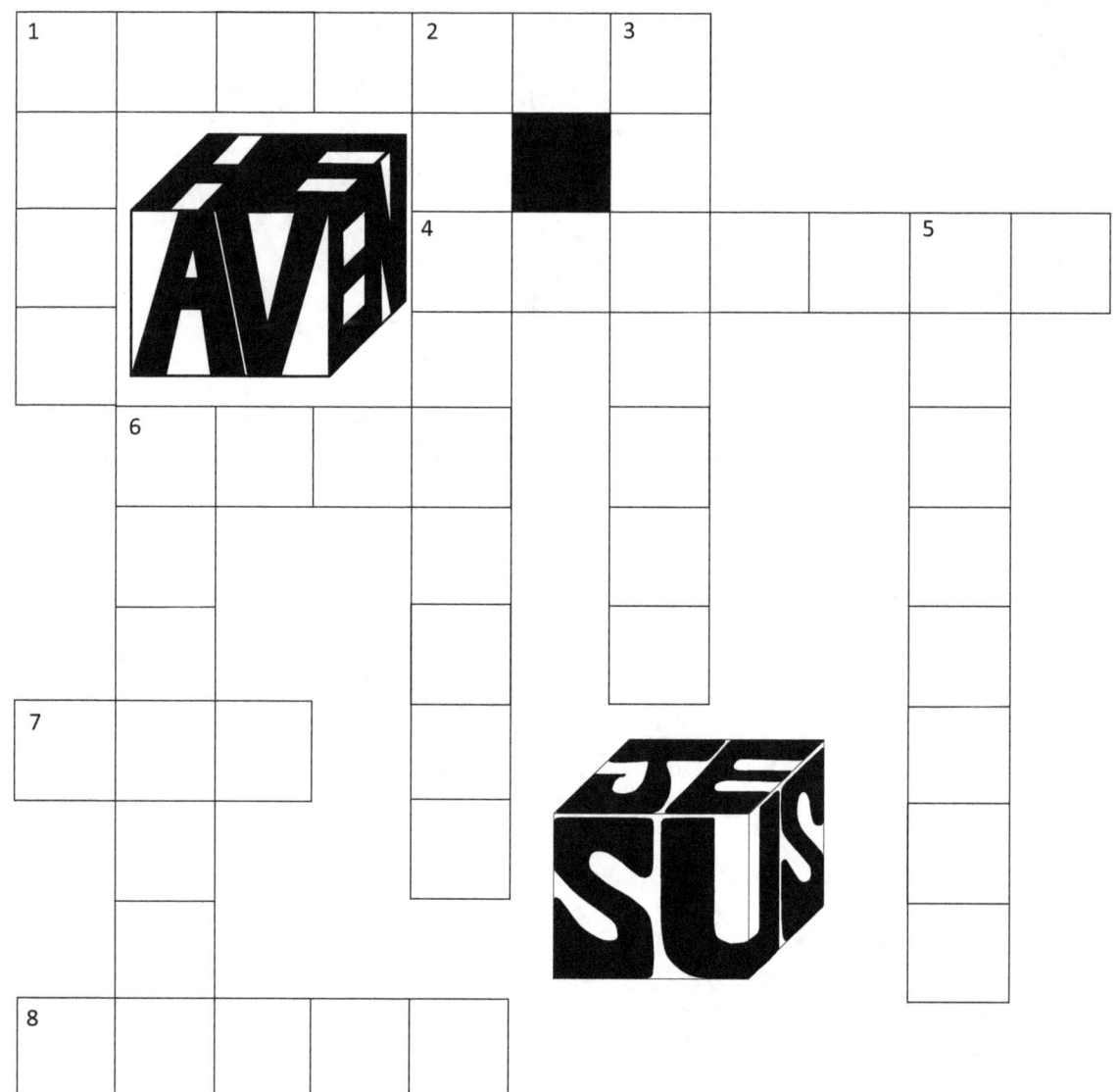

Across:
1. Red insect with black dots
4. Has a shell for a home
6. Peaceful white bird
7. Monkey with no tail
8. Slithers in the grass

Down:
1. King of the jungle
2. Lived in a cocoon
3. Very long neck
5. Very long nose
6. Water mammal

16

Unscramble the Critter's name then match it to the verse that fits it best by drawing a line from the name, to the Critter, and then to the proper verse.

MAR

_____

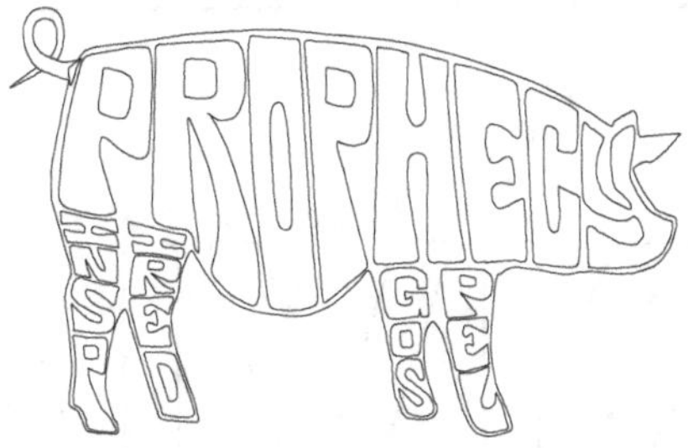

Prophecy Inspired Gospel

Genesis 2:7

BLAM

_____

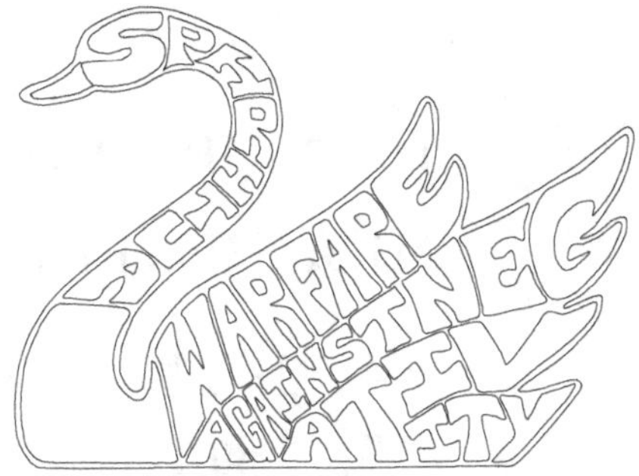

Spiritual Warfare Against Negativity

1 Chronicles 29:11

AWNS

_____

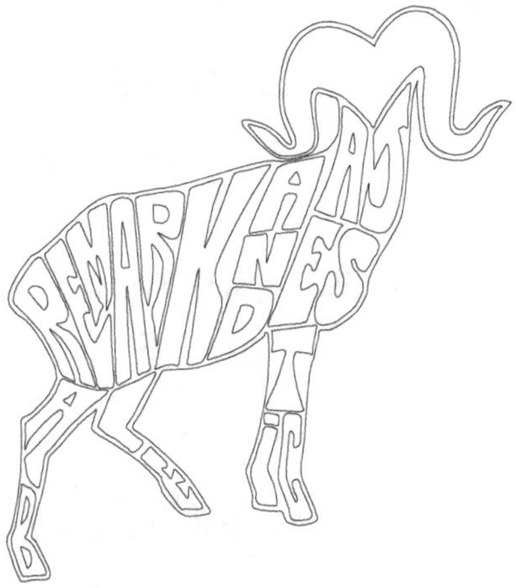

Remarkable And Majestic

Ephesians 6:12

GIP

_____

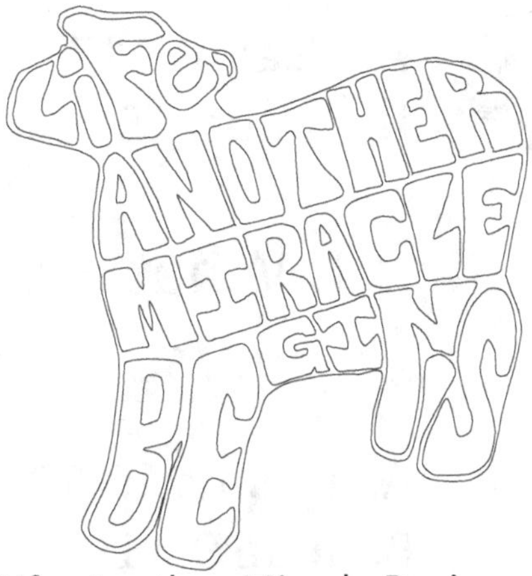

Life, Another Miracle Begins

2 Peter 1:21

17

BIBLE TRIVIA

1. The King James Bible was published in what year?

   A. 1411   C. 1492
   B. 1611   D. 1776

2. What is the longest chapter of the KJV?

   A. Psalms 22   C. Genesis 11
   B. Job 15   D. Psalms 119

3. What is the shortest chapter of the KJV?

   A. Psalms 117   C. Mark 2
   B. Amos 15   D. Numbers 1

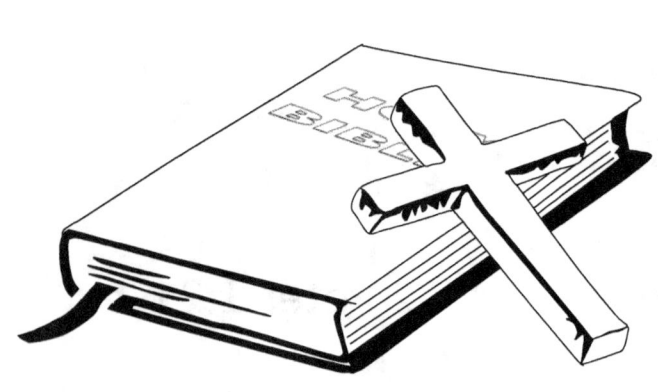

4. What is the longest verse of the KJV?

   A. Psalms 10:10   C. Esther 8:9
   B. Jude 9:11   D. John 3:16

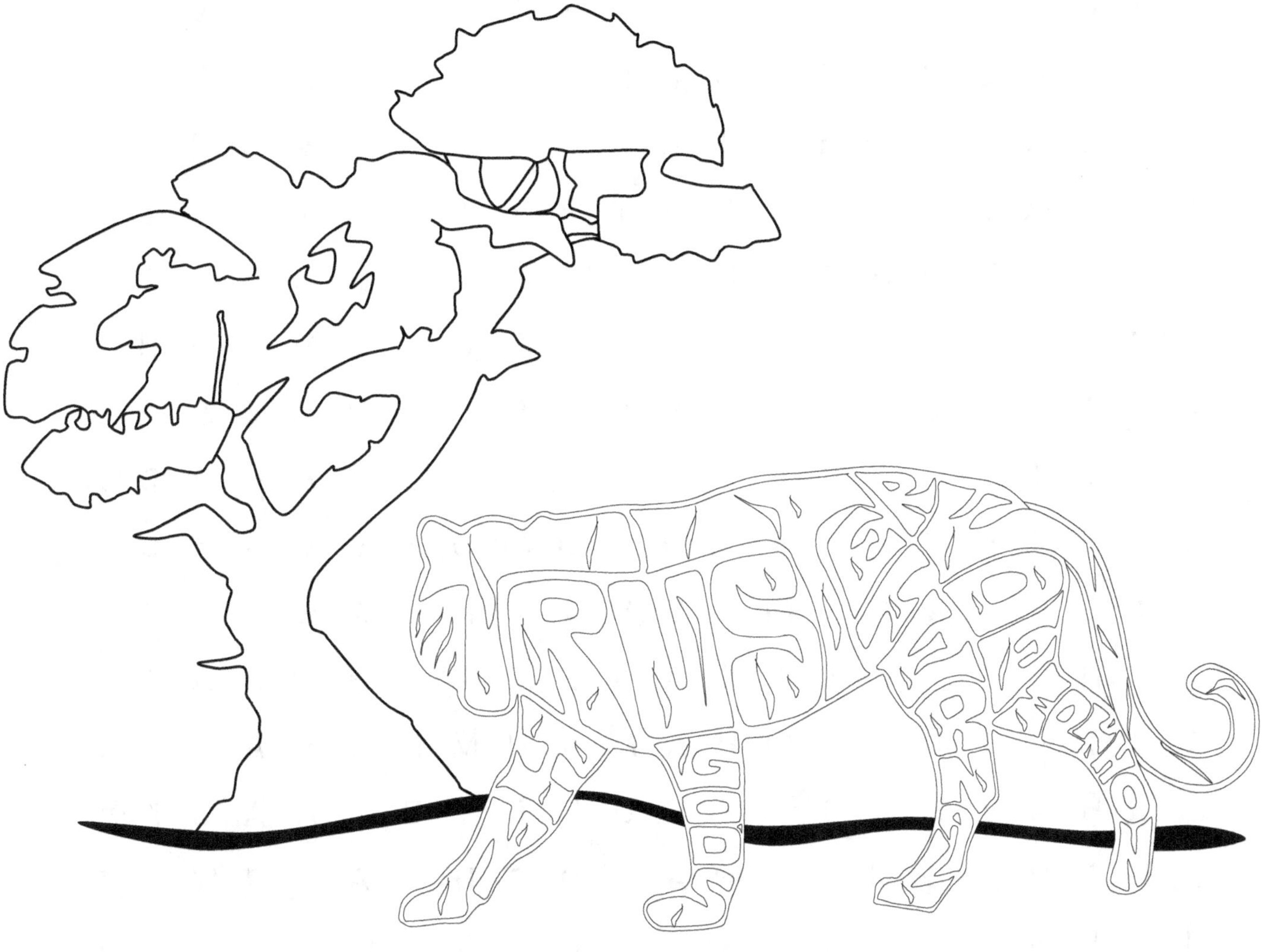

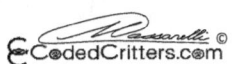

Ephesians 1:7

NAMES OF GOD

Adonai   Elohim   Jehovah-Nissi   Jehovah-Tsidkenu
El Elyon   Jehovah-Jireh   Jehovah-Raah   Yahweh
El Shaddai   Jehovah-   Jehovah-Rapha
El Olam   Mekoddishkem   Jehovah-Shammah

E A R O S E T S I U E L S E L E L J O V M C

J I G E G N O E D G L N J O V J I H A D J E

H J E A J J E H O J A H P A R H A V O H E J

J E E M L E H A V E V Y R N W Z A I A I L S

E H L H V O H E J H O R A D A D J A E J S O

H O E L O L A M E J L R E Z O J E M S U H F

I V A H E V M A N N E S I N E F H T C S A P

A M T J L T A R F I E L A H L E O H H R D A

W E H E C H Z H E R O I O M O N V E S I D E

A Y T H I R A S M J G V J A H I A G T T A C

T E H O S T N S A E A L E C I A H R H A I E

R U T V I L L E M H K M A H M D S E A K E U

H T H A J P A R J E H O E J D H A A O H S

E L I H A C M I I M A J D D H A A T R M E P

N E F N E E R D E R I E R D S L M I H A E L

O O N I P E C O D C T T S M I E M A A S E S

O C E S H L B Y M E J E H O V S A M V N O O

M E S S V O T U Y A H W E H O H H J O V H R

T O T I E E R B C J A H V O H E J K H T P A

H E F A T H J E H O V A H T S I D K E N U V

N O Y L E L E E V T H R N U A N H T N J M O J

B C J D J W W N A E E D E M R E O O J T N U

20

LETTER SCRAMBLE

Using the Letter Key Code in the box below change the letters to solve the Bible verse then circle the correct verse.

A = Z	H = S	O = L	V = E
B = Y	I = R	P = K	W = D
C = X	J = Q	Q = J	X = C
D = W	K = P	R = I	Y = B
E = V	L = O	S = H	Z = A
F = U	M = N	T = G	
G = T	N = M	U = F	

‾‾ ‾‾‾‾ ‾‾‾‾ ‾‾‾‾ ‾‾‾‾ ‾‾ ‾‾‾‾‾‾
DV PMLD DSZG IVZO OLEV RH YVXZFHV

‾‾‾‾‾ ‾‾‾‾ ‾‾ ‾‾‾ ‾‾‾‾ ‾‾‾‾‾ ‾‾
QVHFH TZEV FK SRH ORUV ULIFH. HL

‾‾ ‾‾‾‾ ‾‾‾‾‾ ‾‾ ‾‾‾‾ ‾‾ ‾‾‾ ‾‾‾‾‾
DV ZOHL LFTSG GL TREV FK LFI OREVH

‾‾‾ ‾‾‾ ‾‾‾‾‾‾‾‾ ‾‾‾ ‾‾‾‾‾‾‾
ULI LFI YILGSVIH ZMW HRHGVIH

John 3:16   1 John 3:16   2 John 3:16   3 John 3:16

21

CRITTER TRAIL

Trace the critter's trail from start to end without lifting the marker, without crossing any line, and without retracing any segment.

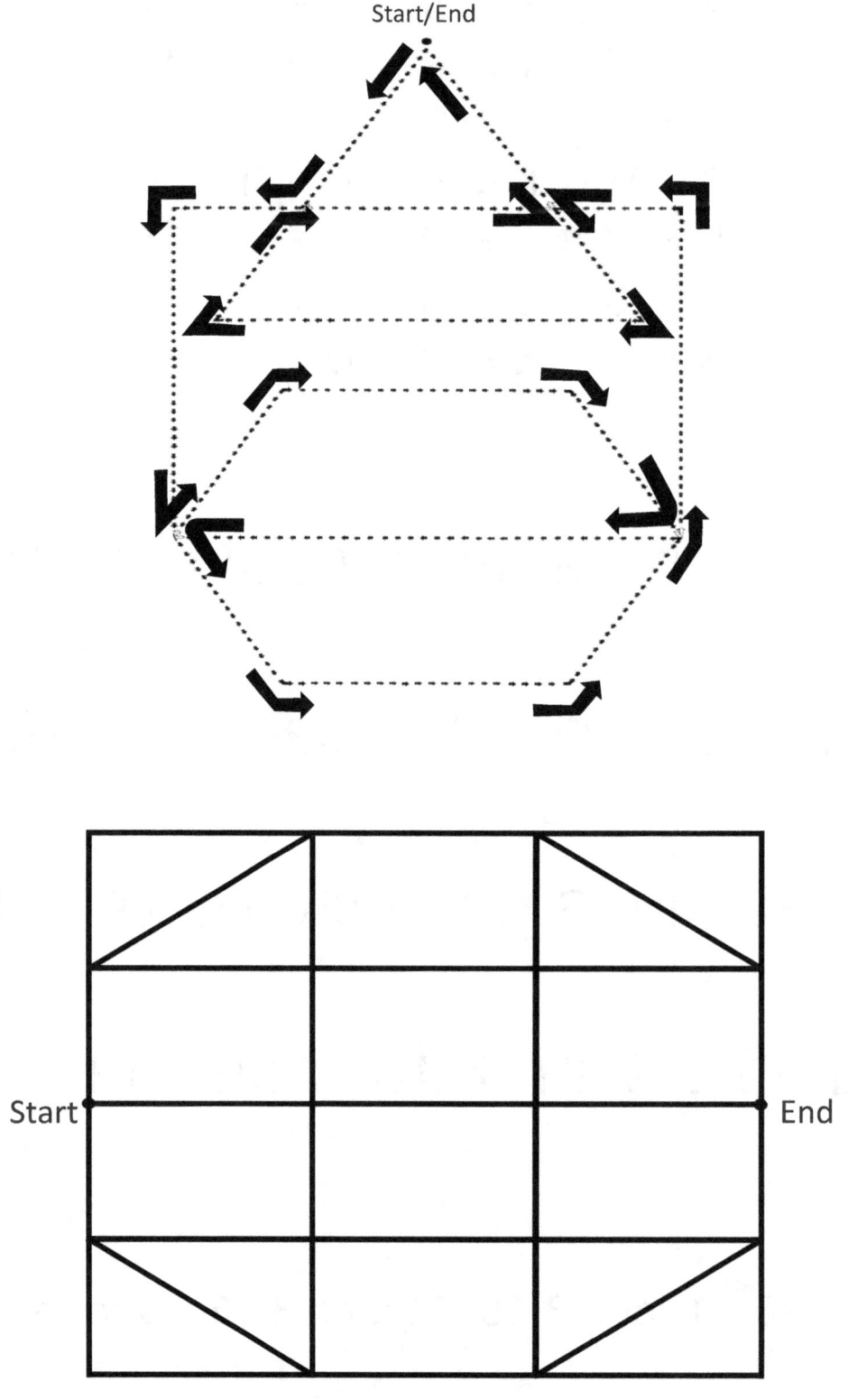

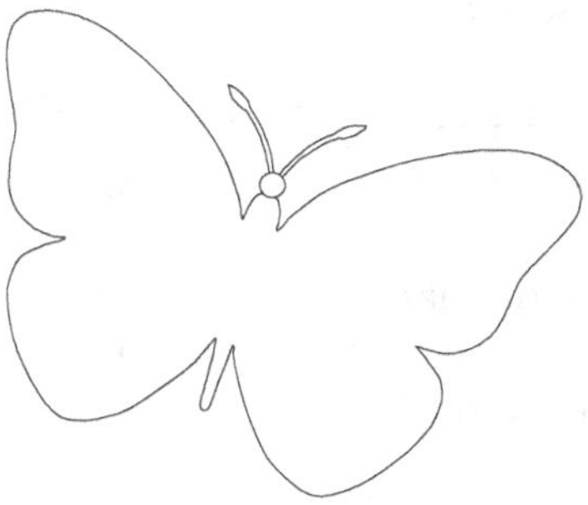

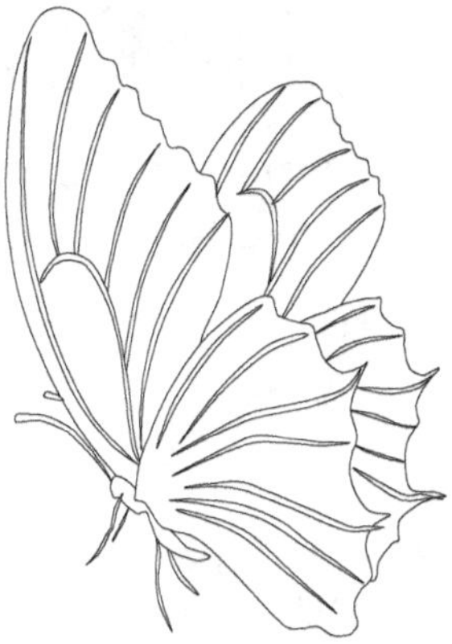

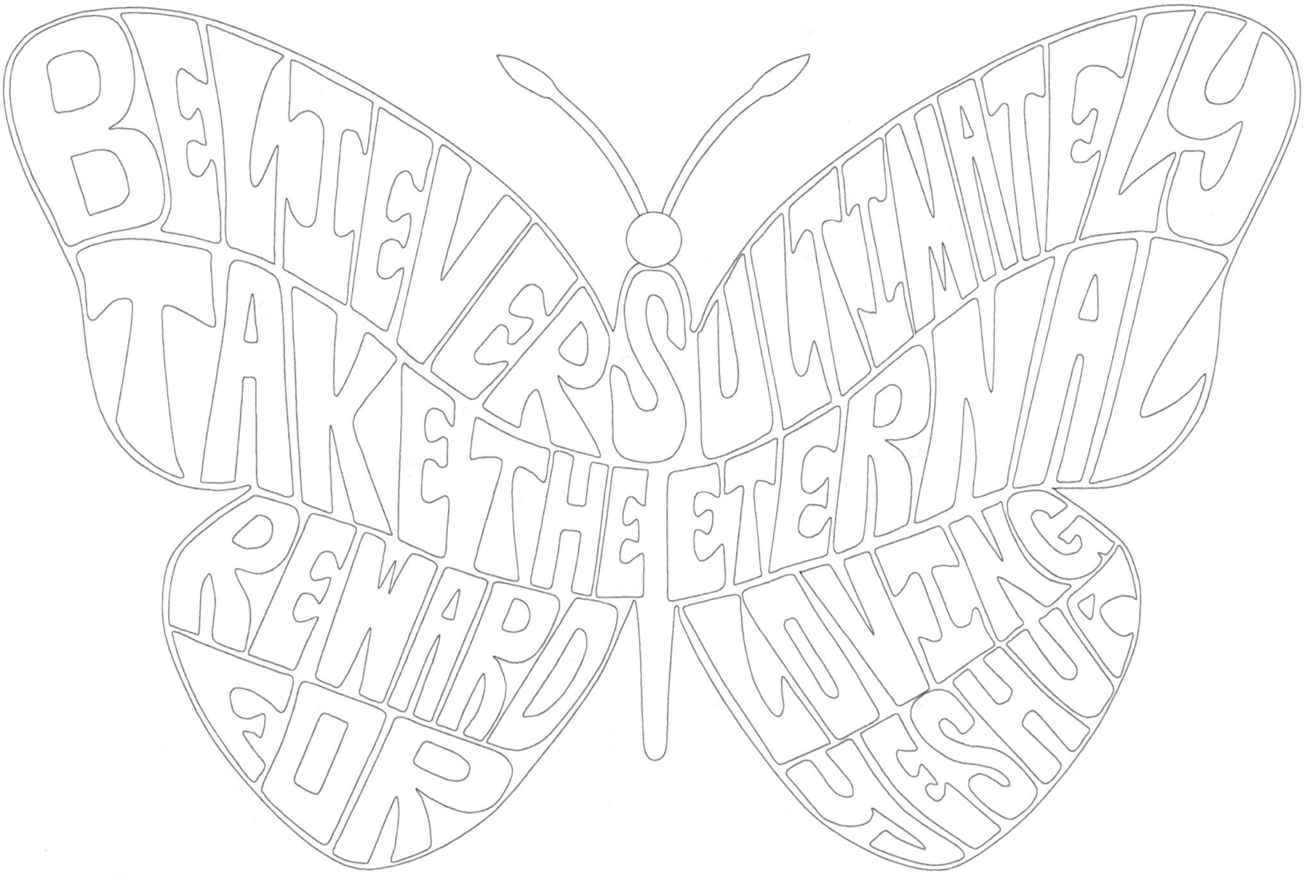

Believers ultimately take the eternal reward for loving Yeshua

Colossians 3:24

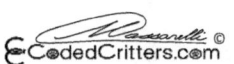

MAP DIRECTIONS

Using the Compass 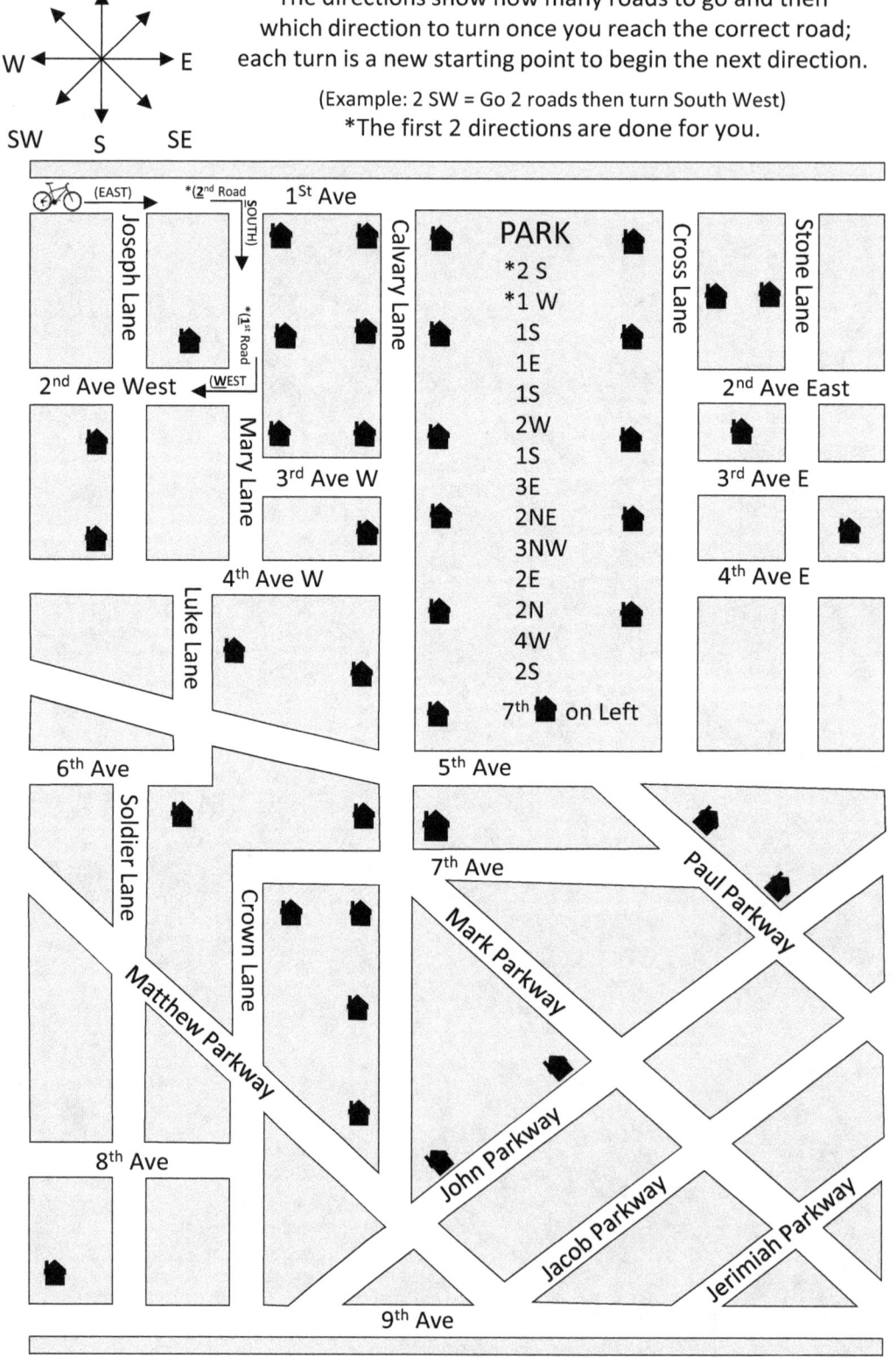 below and the directions in the PARK ride the bike to the correct house 🏠 and color the road as you go.

NW   N   NE

W   E

SW   S   SE

The directions show how many roads to go and then which direction to turn once you reach the correct road; each turn is a new starting point to begin the next direction.

(Example: 2 SW = Go 2 roads then turn South West)
*The first 2 directions are done for you.

PARK
- *2 S
- *1 W
- 1S
- 1E
- 1S
- 2W
- 1S
- 3E
- 2NE
- 3NW
- 2E
- 2N
- 4W
- 2S
- 7th 🏠 on Left

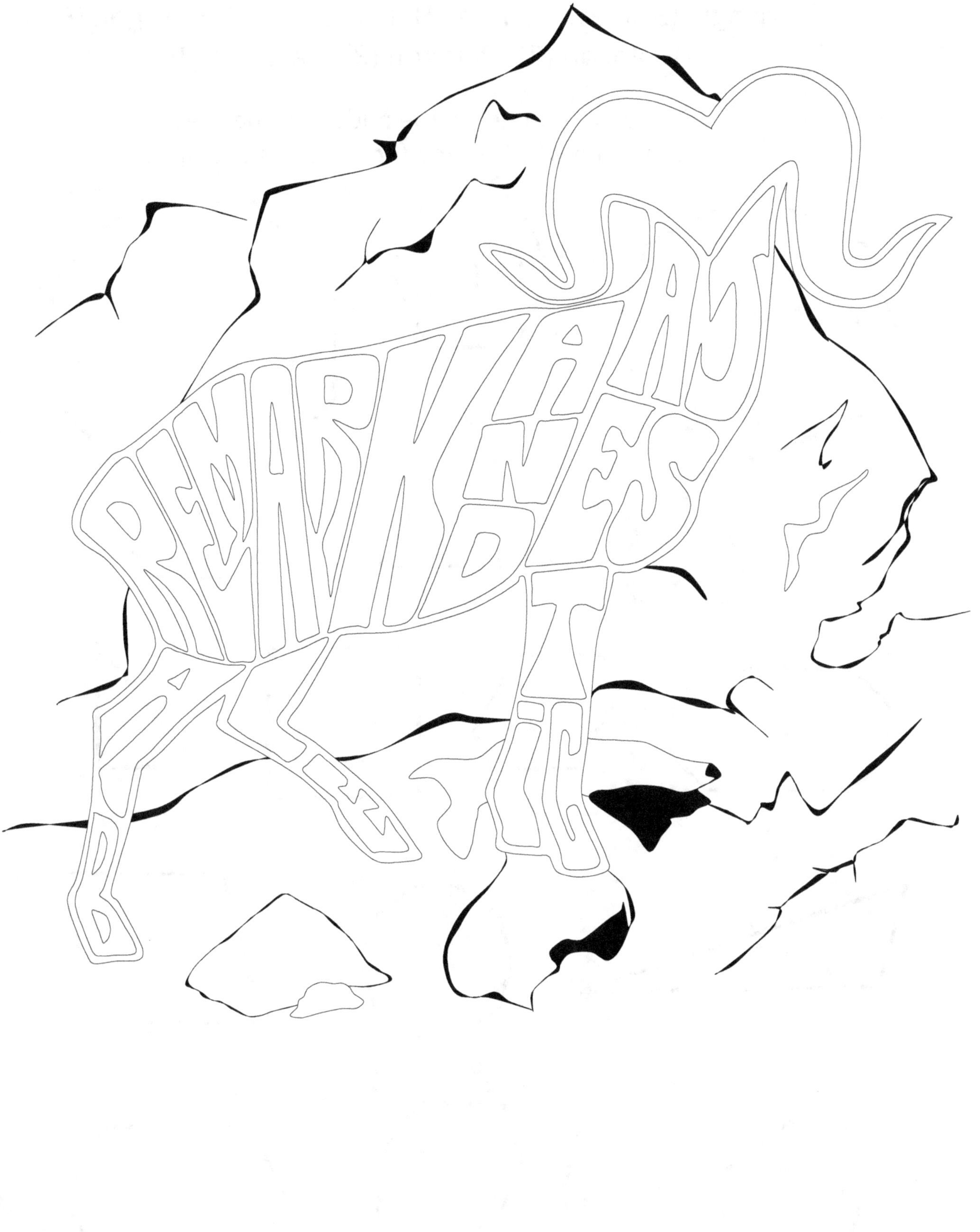

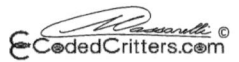

1 Chronicles 29:11

SHAPES FINDER

Triangle (3 sides) Square (4) Pentagon (5) Hexagon (6)
Heptagon (7) Octagon (8) Decagon (10)

Write the number in the middle of the shape
to indicate which shape (how many sides) it is.

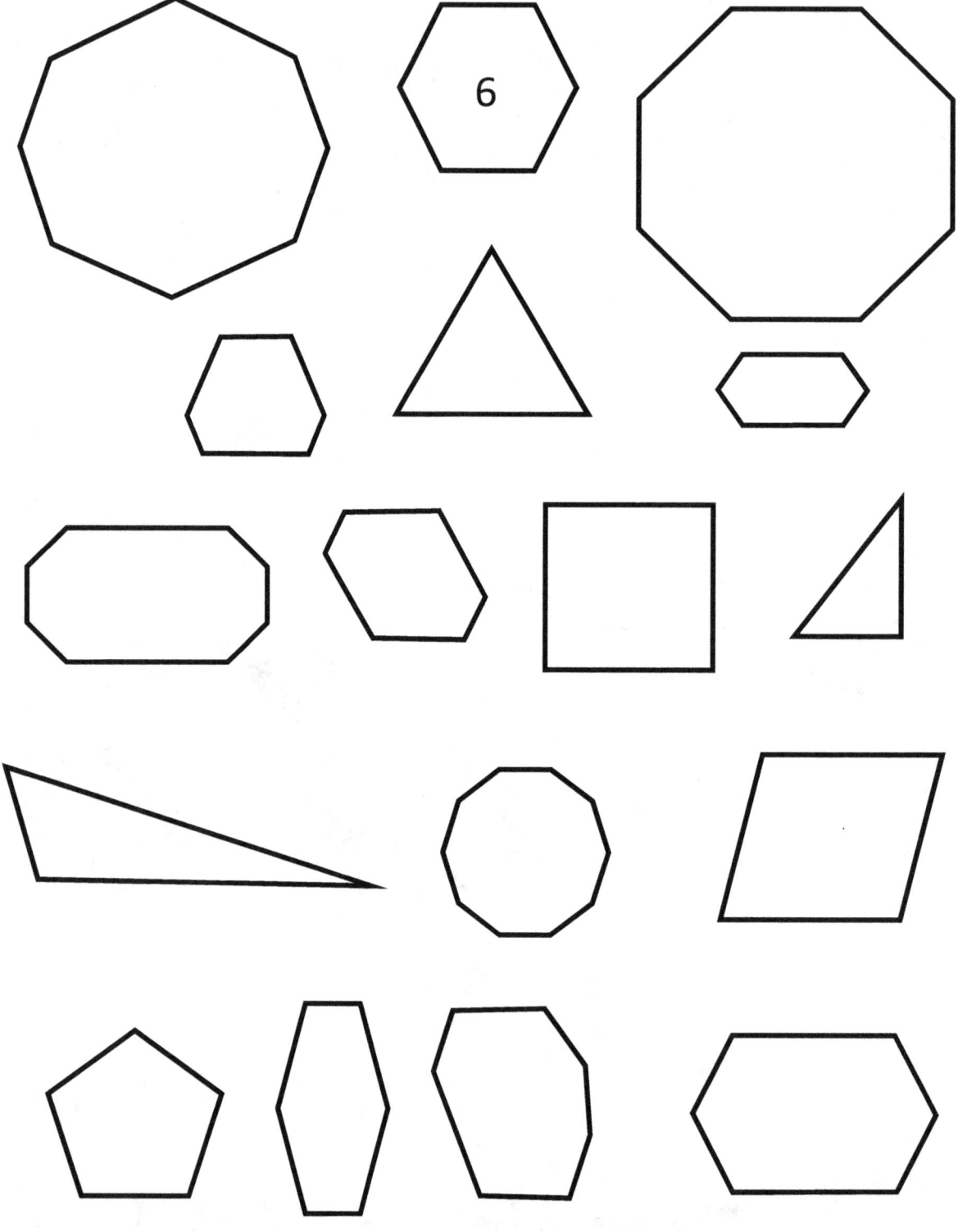

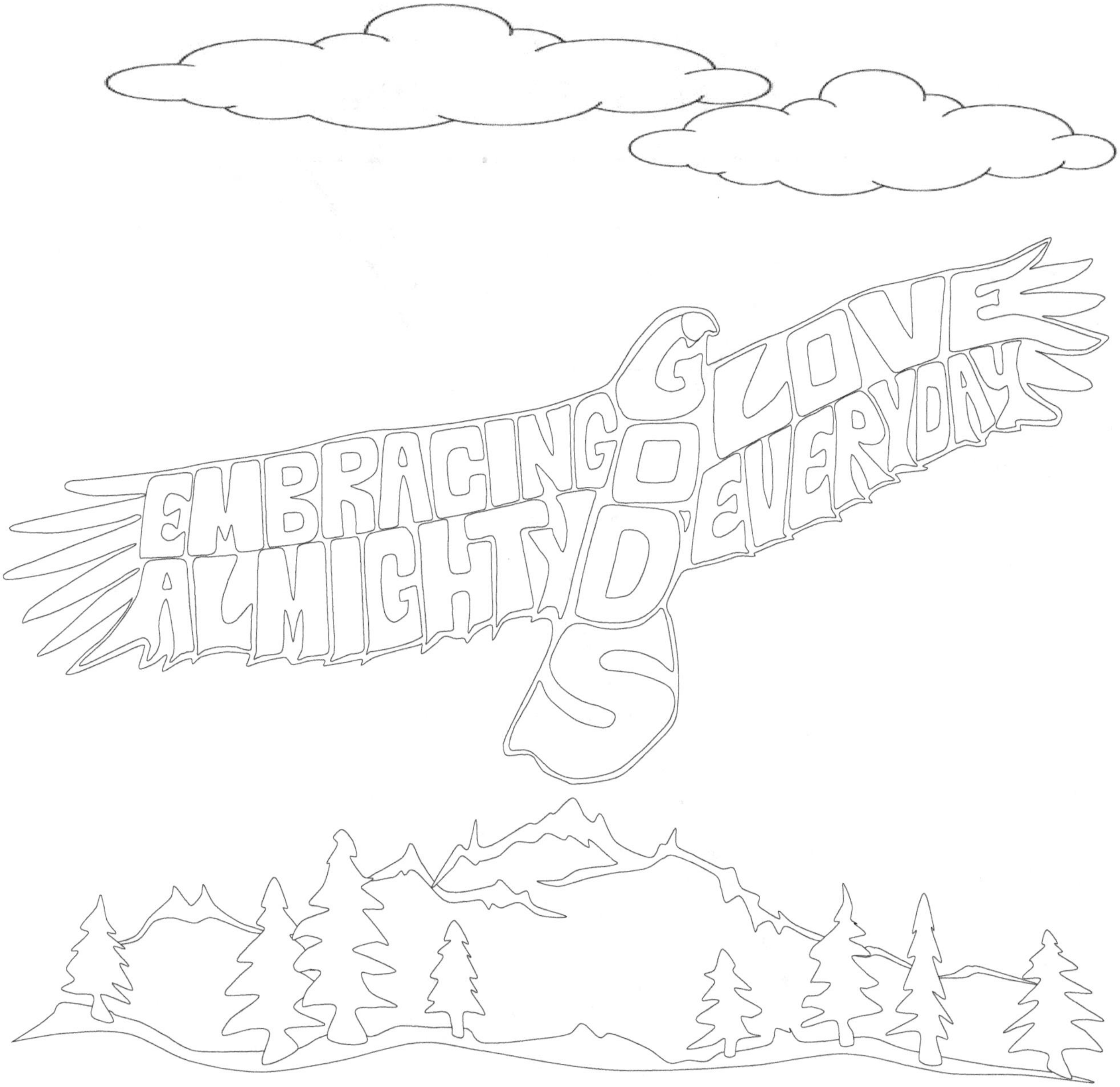

EMBRACING GOD'S ALMIGHTY LOVE EVERYDAY

1 John 4:16

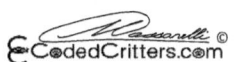

SHAPE FINDER
How many Triangles 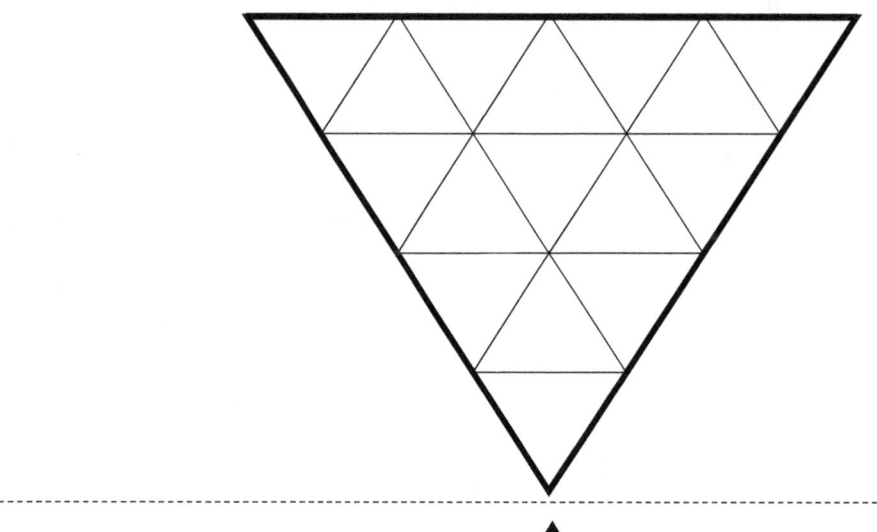 can you find in the puzzle?

A. 17   C. 27   E. 36
B. 21   D. 33   F. Other

A. 22   C. 65   E. 88
B. 44   D. 72   F. Other

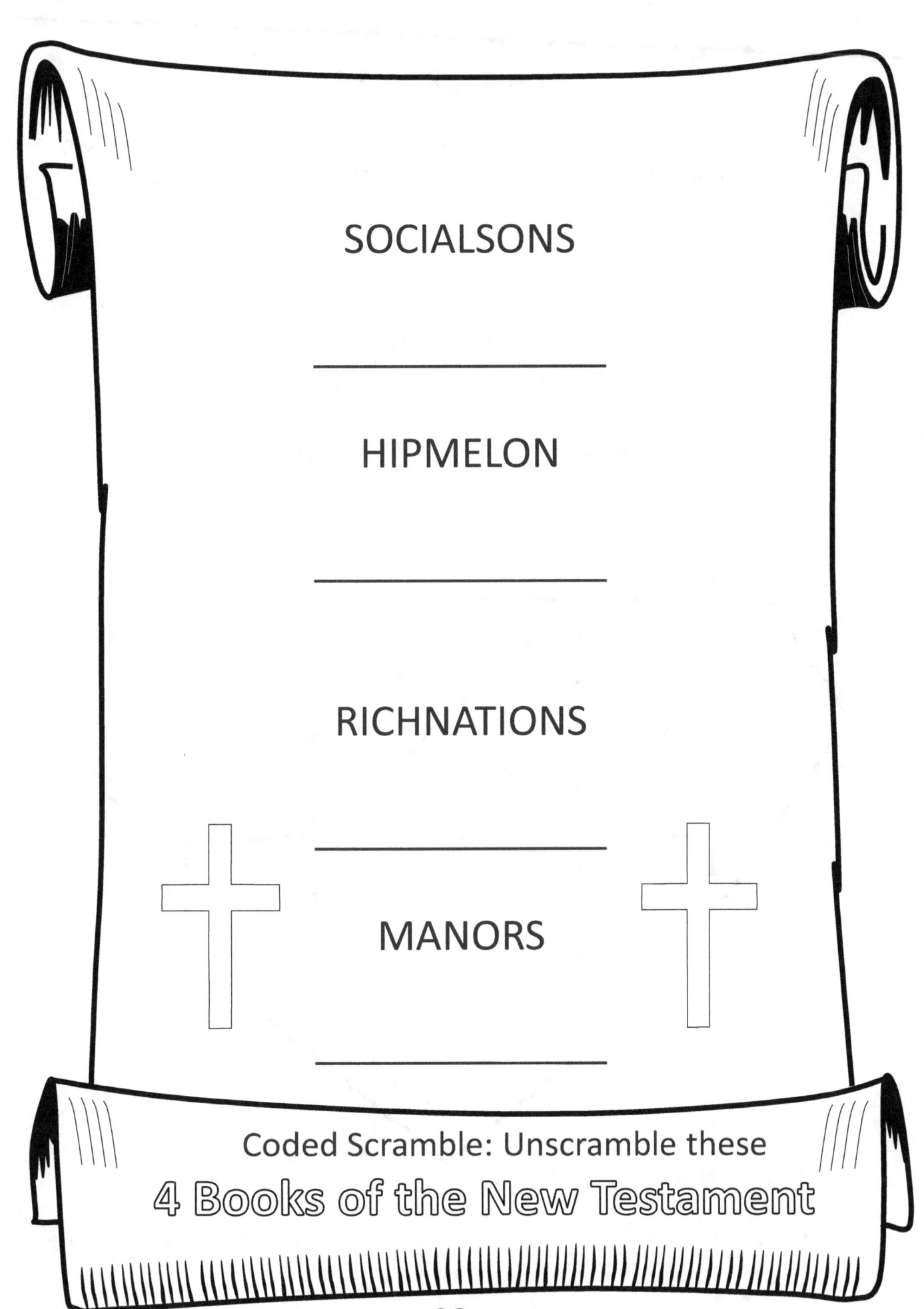

SOCIALSONS

_____

HIPMELON

_____

RICHNATIONS

_____

MANORS

_____

CRITTER TRAIL

Trace the critter's trail from start to end without lifting the marker,
without crossing any line, and without retracing any segment.

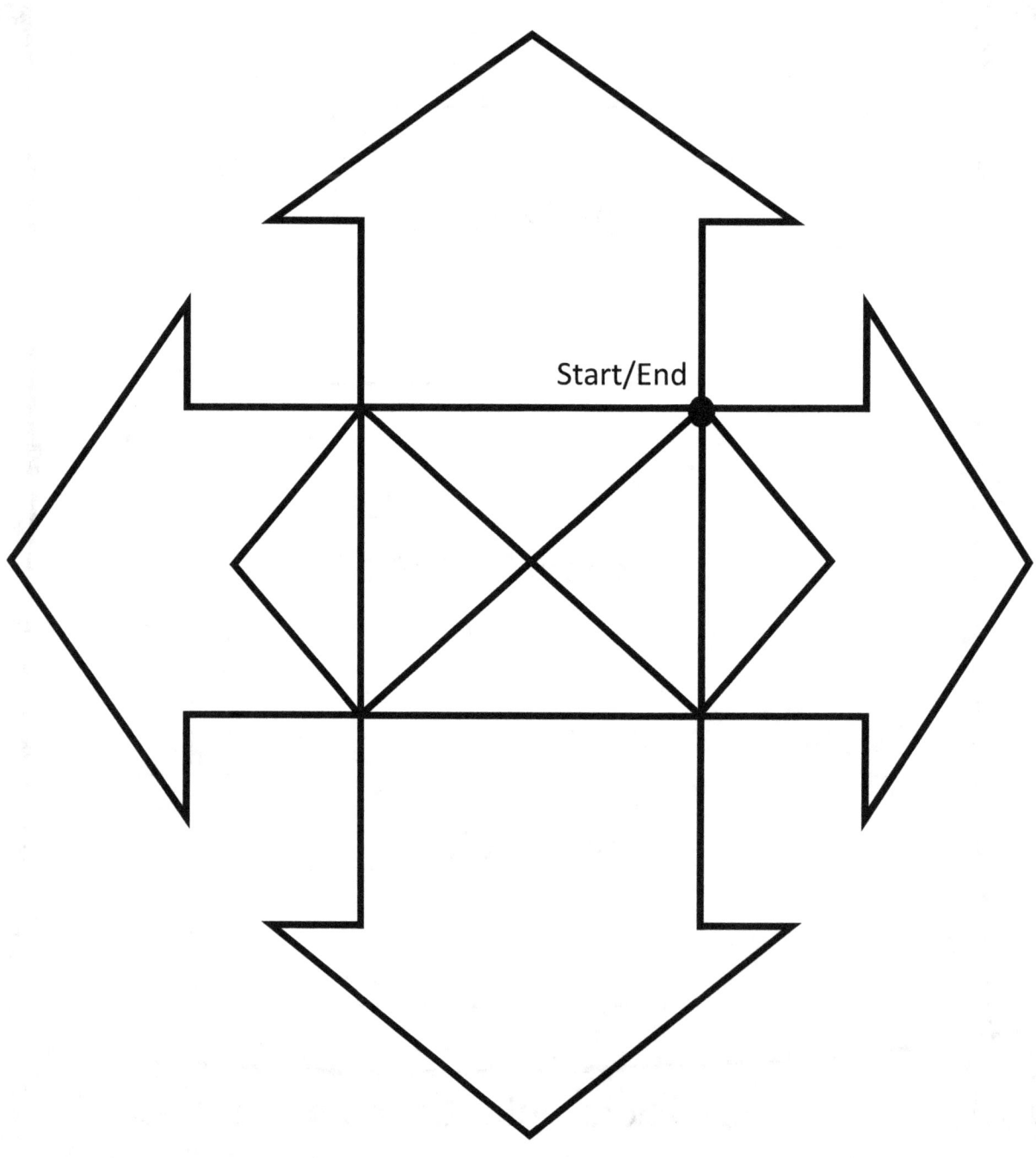

Start/End

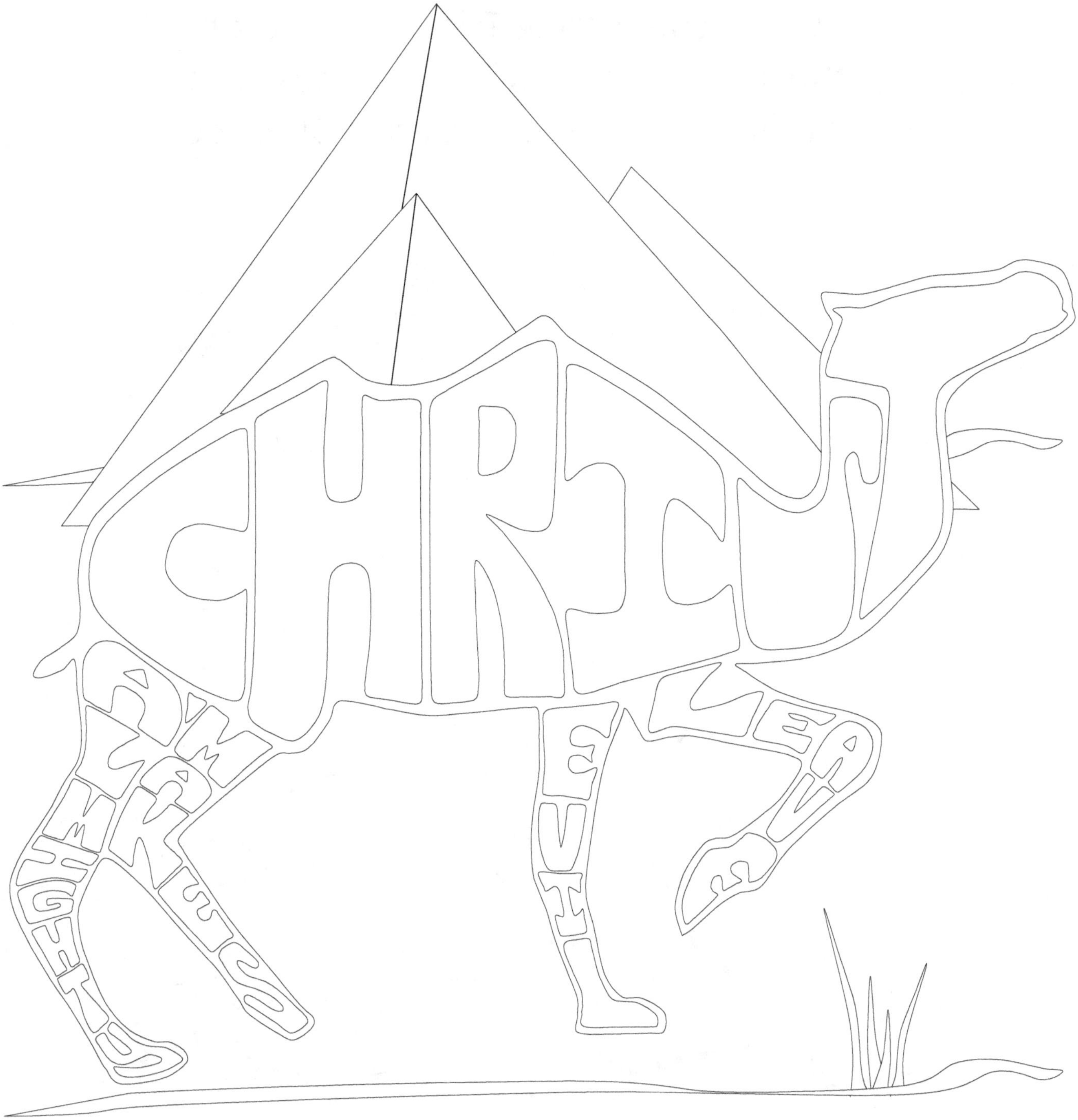

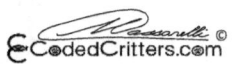

Luke 10:17

HIDDEN CUBE / HIDDEN CROSS
Color 2 connecting Triangles △▽ or ⊖ the same color 3 different times with 3 different colors to create a 3D Cube ▢.

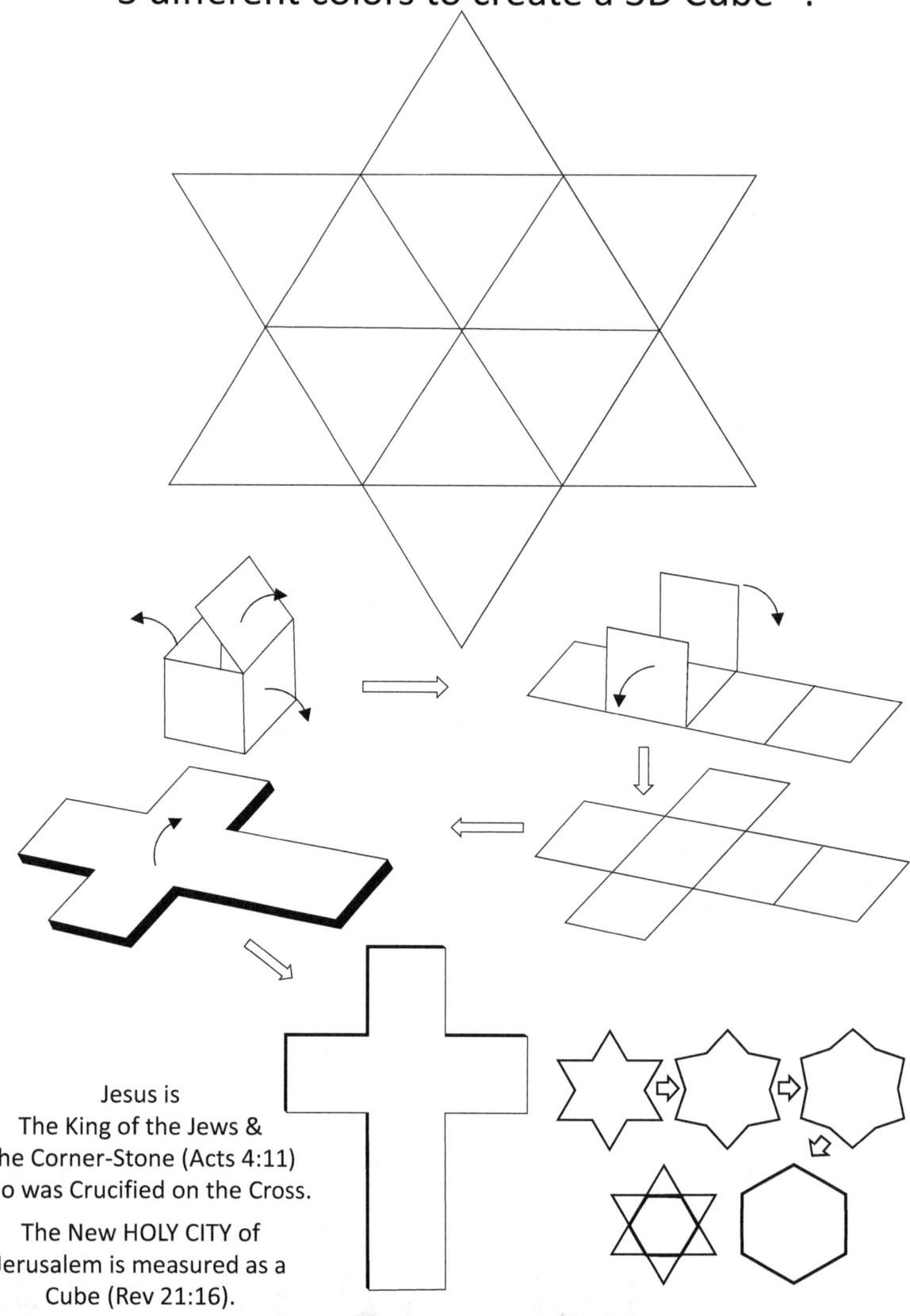

Jesus is
The King of the Jews &
The Corner-Stone (Acts 4:11)
who was Crucified on the Cross.

The New HOLY CITY of
Jerusalem is measured as a
Cube (Rev 21:16).

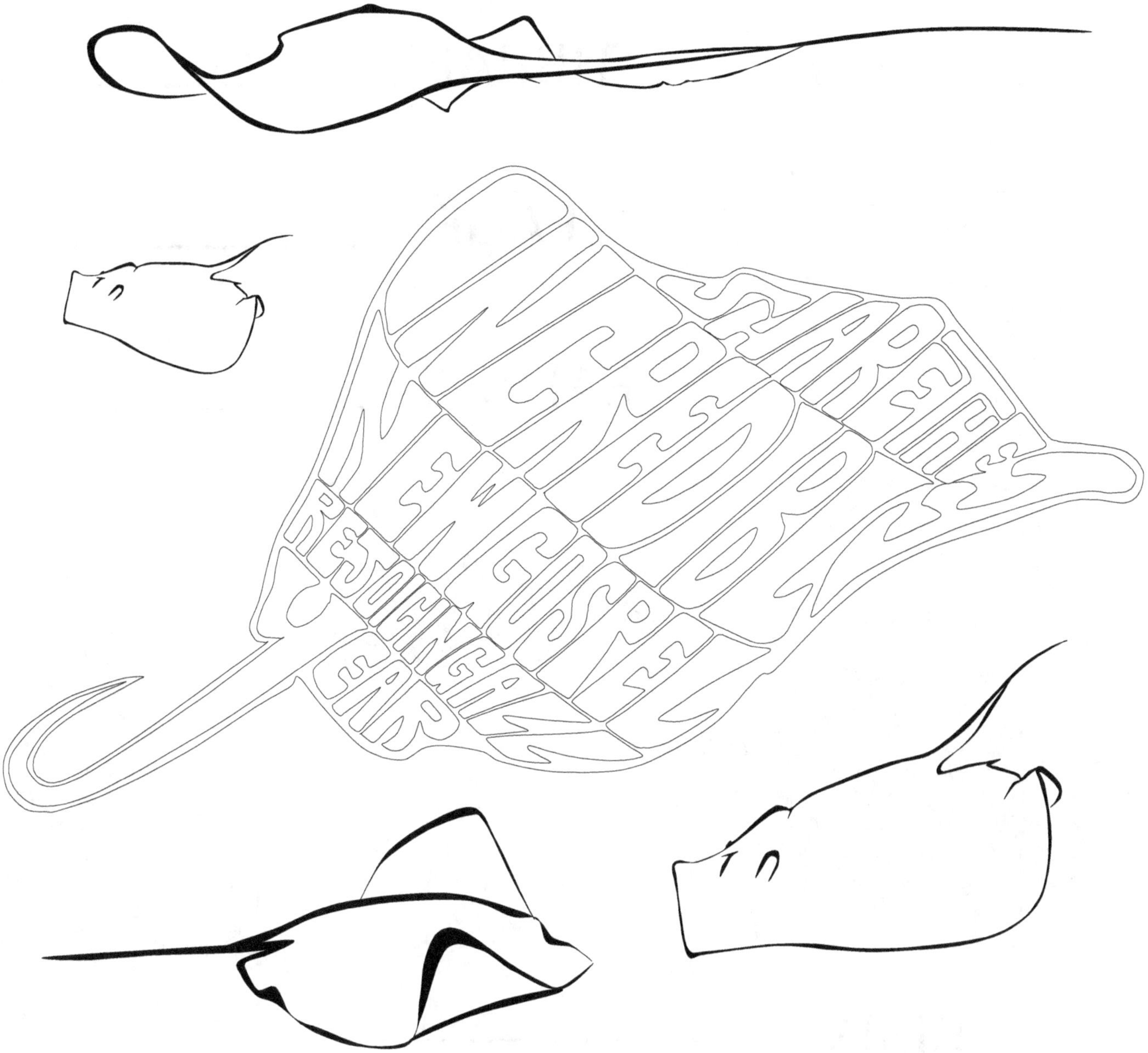

Mark 16:15

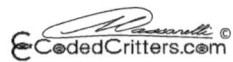

UNSCRAMBLE THE CRITTERS

TIBRAB _____

LEAGE _____

EAFRIGF _____

RIBD _____

HPAENLTE _____

EPA _____

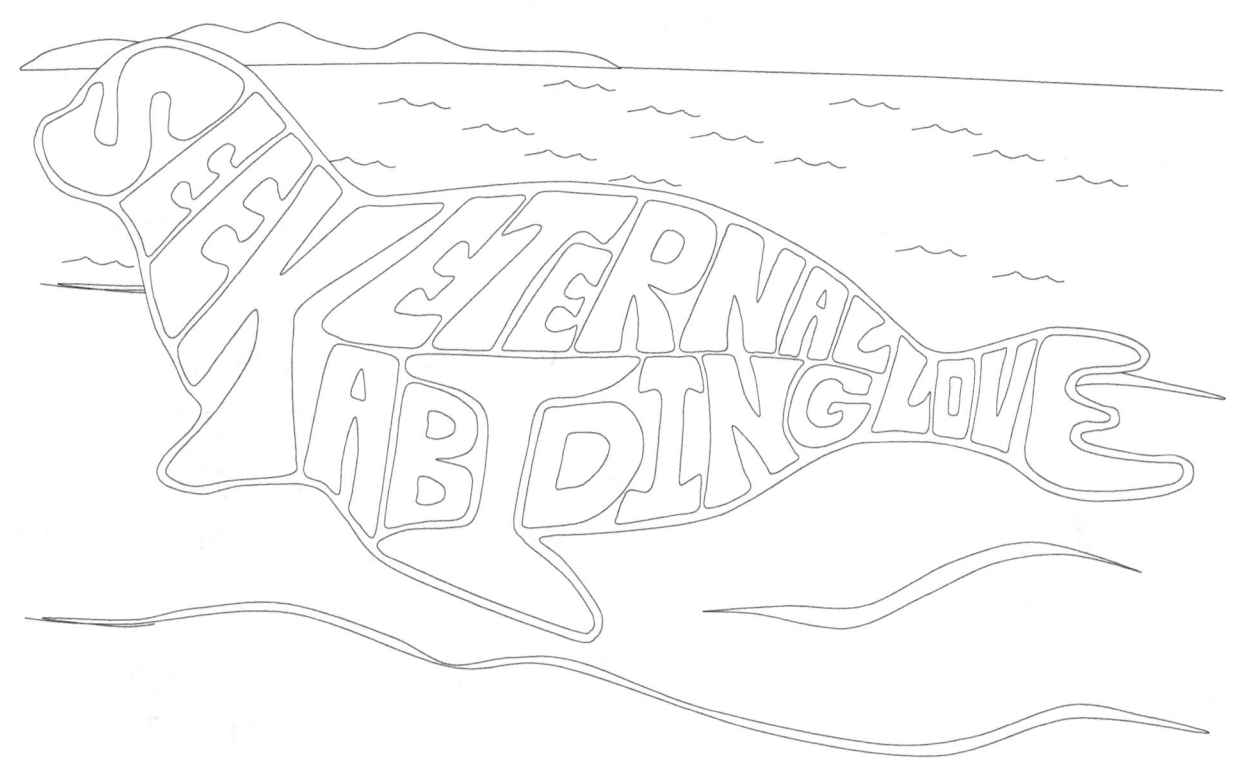

Deuteronomy 4:29

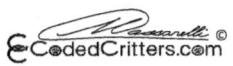

BIBLE TRIVIA

1. Which are the 2 shortest verses of the KJV?

A. 1 Chron 1:25 & John 11:35   C. Esther 8:9 & 1 Chron 1:25

B. 1 Thes 5:16 & 1 Chron 1:25   D. John 11:35 & 1 Thes 5:16

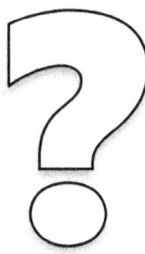

2. What is the middle book of the Old Testament?

A. Proverbs   C. Job

B. Psalms   D. Ecclesiastes

3. What is the middle book of the New Testament?

A. 1 Thessalonians   C. 2 Thessalonians

B. Colossians   D. 1 Timothy

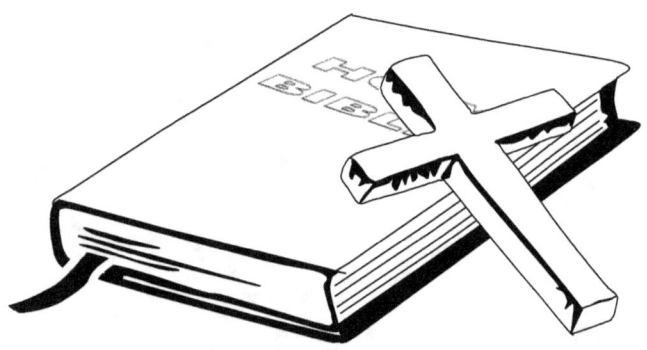

4. How many books are in the Bible?

A. 60   C. 39

B. 66   D. 27

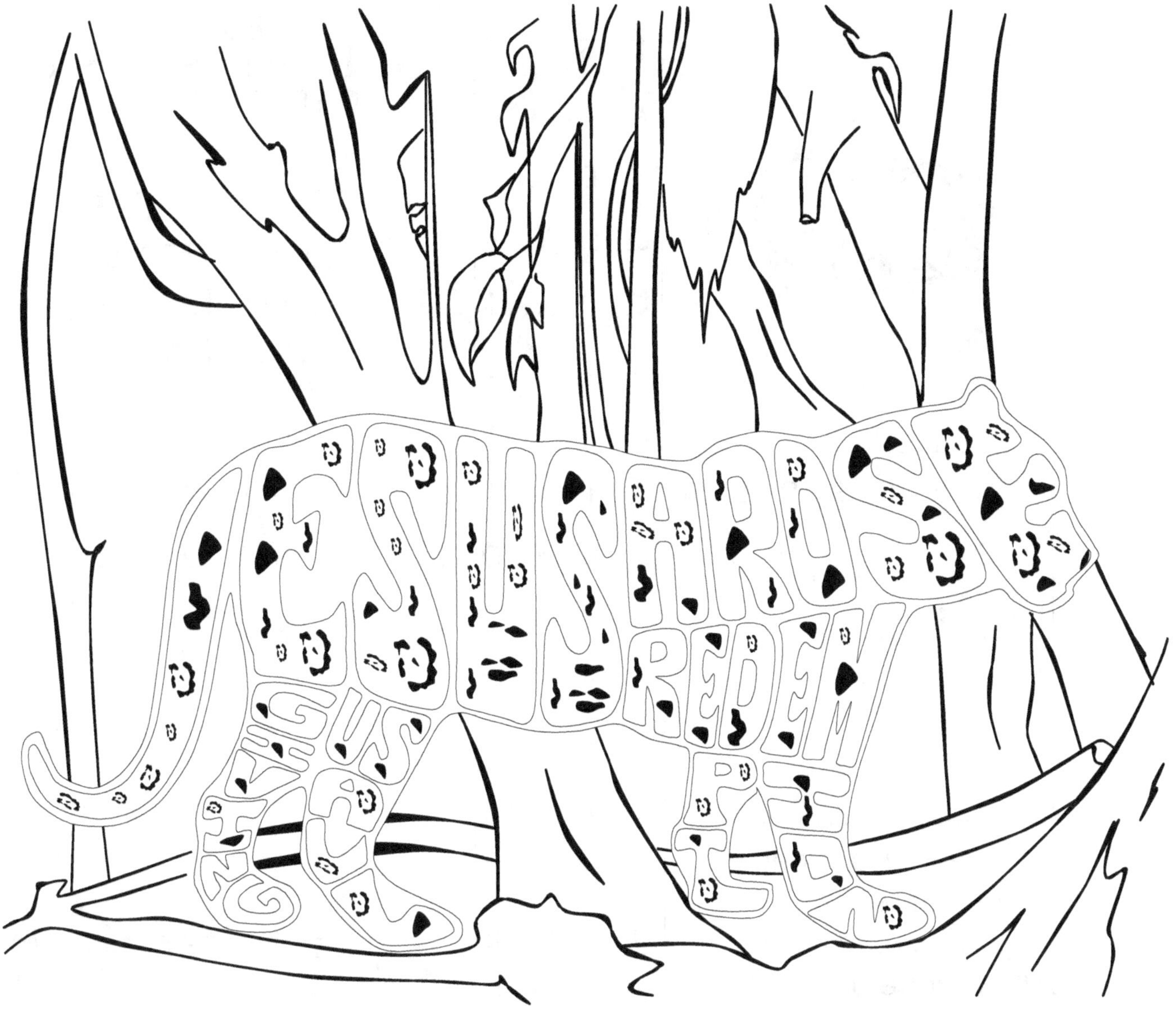

2 Corinthians 4:14

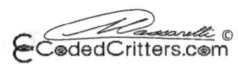

CODED CROSS WORD PUZZLE
Find and trace along
"The Lord's Prayer"

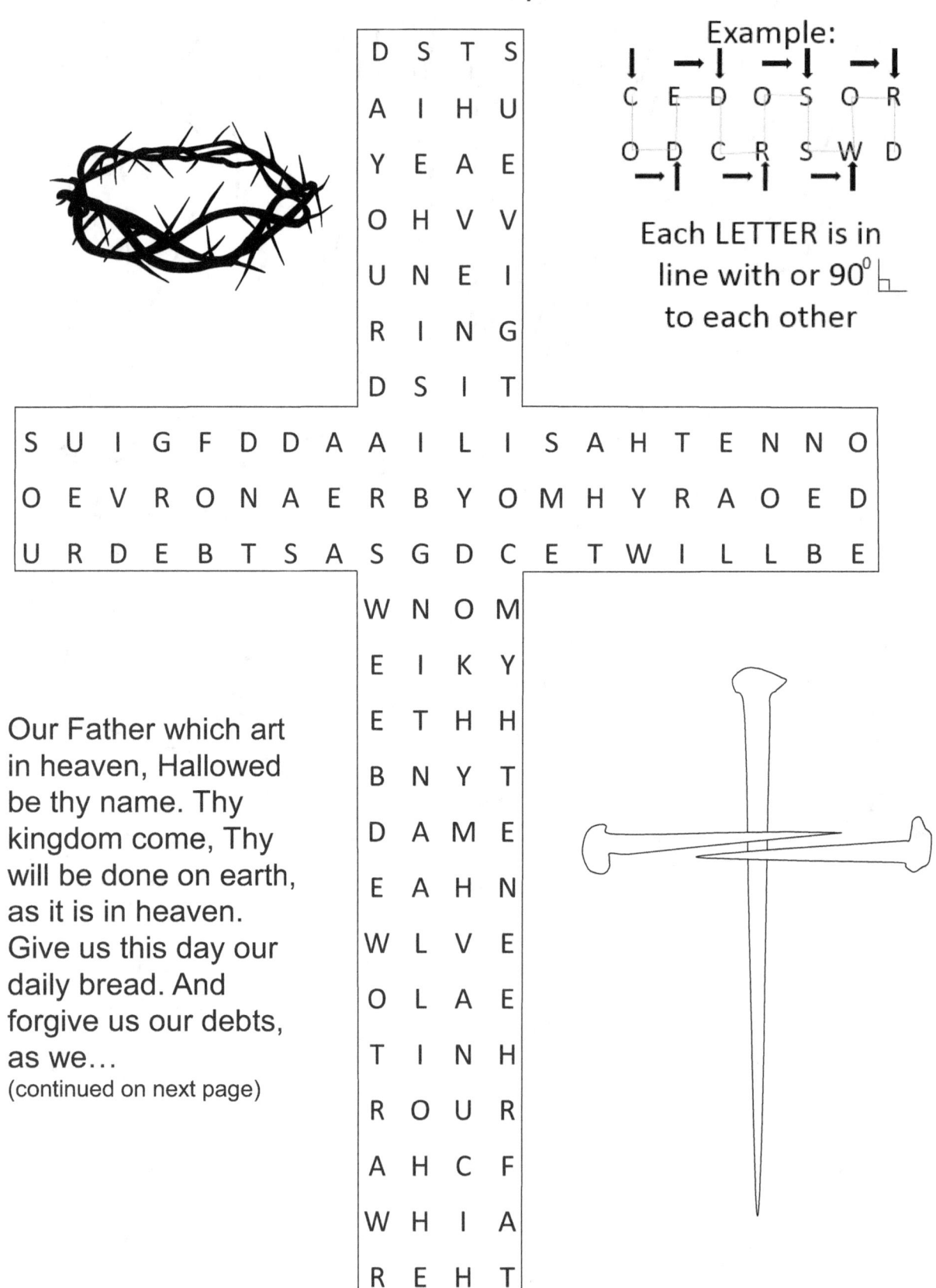

Example:

C E D O S O R
O D C R S W D

Each LETTER is in
line with or 90° ⌐
to each other

Our Father which art
in heaven, Hallowed
be thy name. Thy
kingdom come, Thy
will be done on earth,
as it is in heaven.
Give us this day our
daily bread. And
forgive us our debts,
as we…
(continued on next page)

The 1st half of The Lord's Prayer is written in this cross with one continuous
line without crossing over any letter twice. Trace it without lifting the marker.

CODED CROSS WORD PUZZLE
Find and trace along
"The Lord's Prayer"

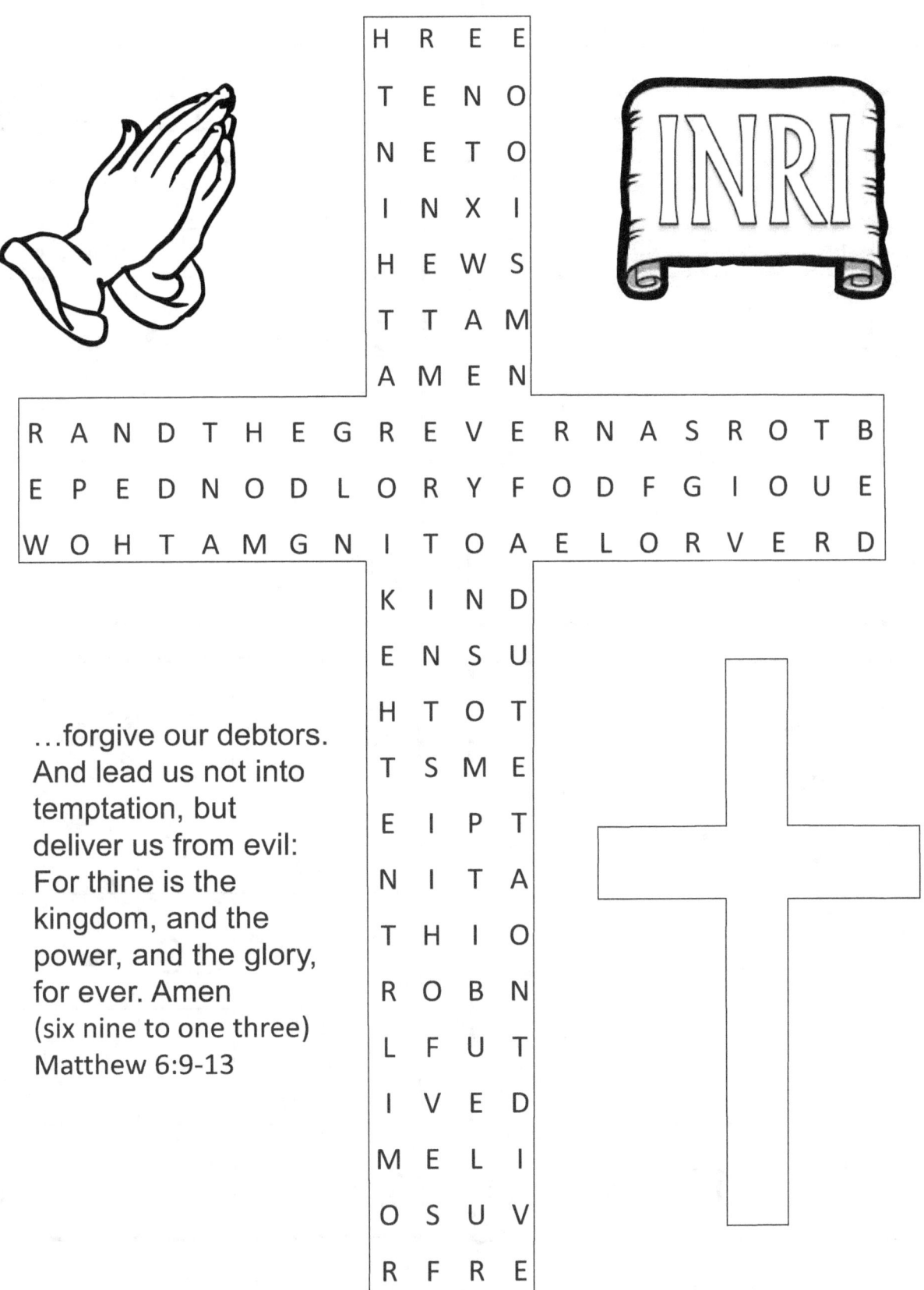

```
H R E E
T E N O
N E T O
I N X I
H E W S
T T A M
A M E N
```

```
R A N D T H E G R E V E R N A S R O T B
E P E D N O D L O R Y F O D F G I O U E
W O H T A M G N I T O A E L O R V E R D
```

```
K I N D
E N S U
H T O T
T S M E
E I P T
N I T A
T H I O
R O B N
L F U T
I V E D
M E L I
O S U V
R F R E
```

…forgive our debtors.
And lead us not into
temptation, but
deliver us from evil:
For thine is the
kingdom, and the
power, and the glory,
for ever. Amen
(six nine to one three)
Matthew 6:9-13

The 2nd half of The Lord's Prayer is written in this cross with one continuous
line without crossing over any letter twice. Trace it without lifting the marker.

CODED NUMBER LOGIC

Find the missing numbers

8	+	3	=	
+		+		+
14	+	8	=	
=		=		=
	+		=	

	+	18	=	36
+		+		+
2	+		=	
=		=		=
20	+		=	44

5	+		=	
+		+		+
	+		=	11
=		=		=
7	+	13	=	20

6	+		=	15
+		+		+
	+	10	=	
=		=		=
14	+		=	33

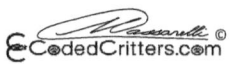

Luke 24:6

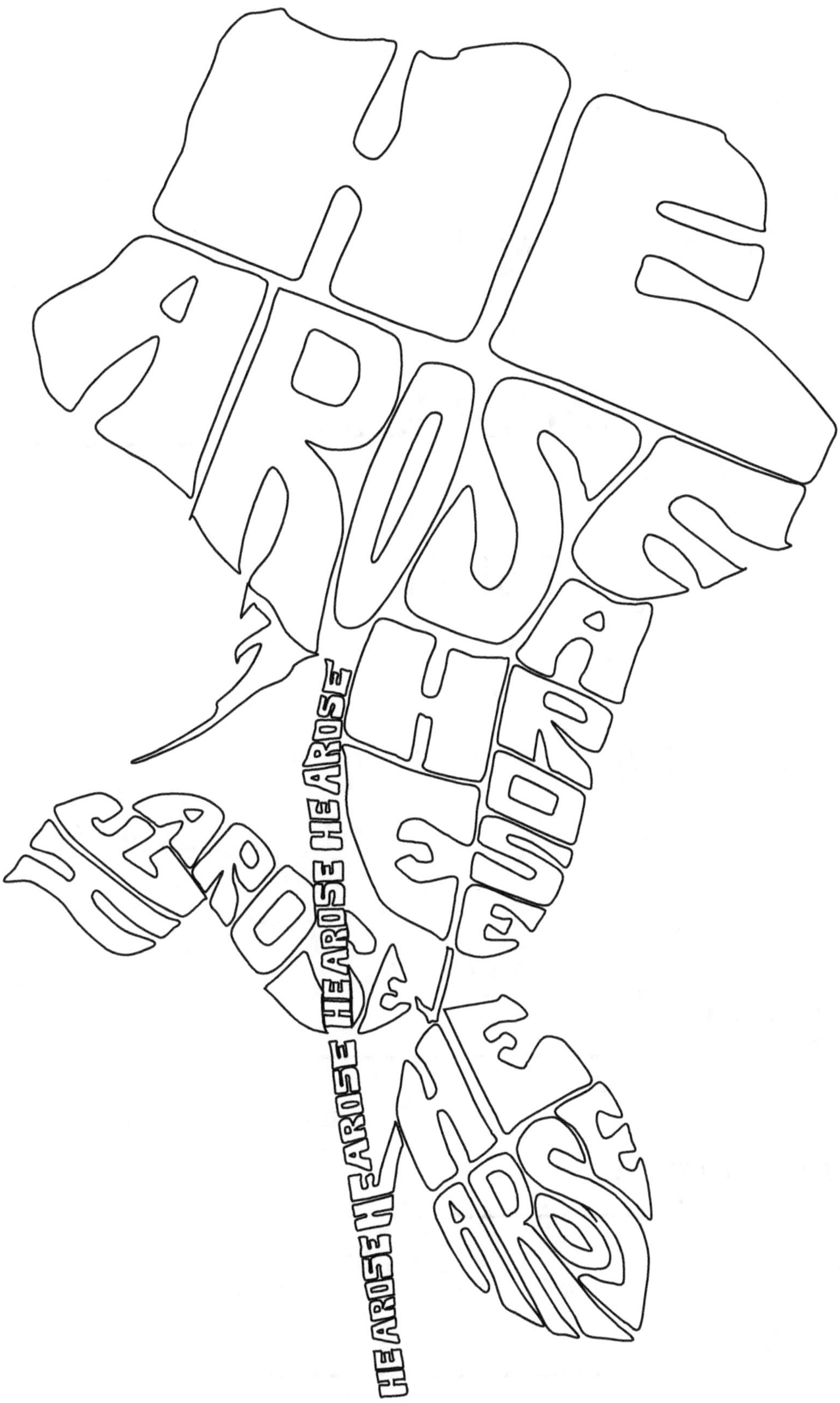

UNSCRAMBLE THE CRITTERS

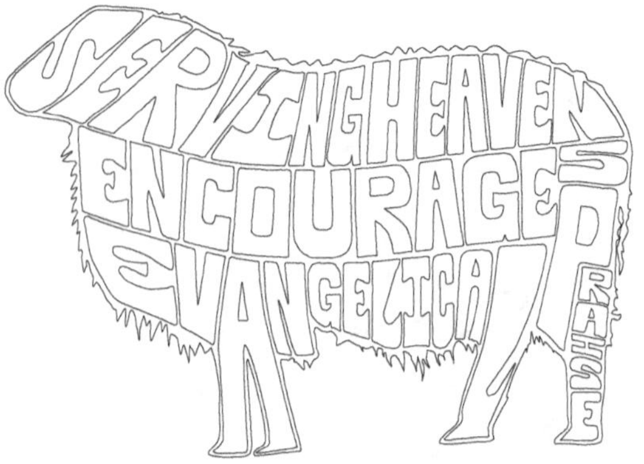

NOIL

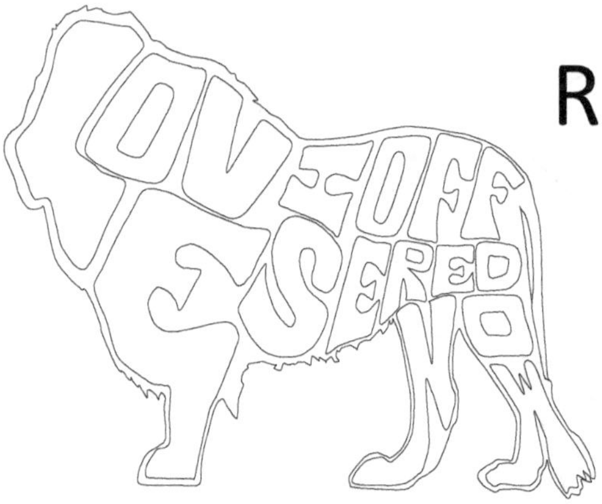

_____

RAGONKAO

_____

PSHEE

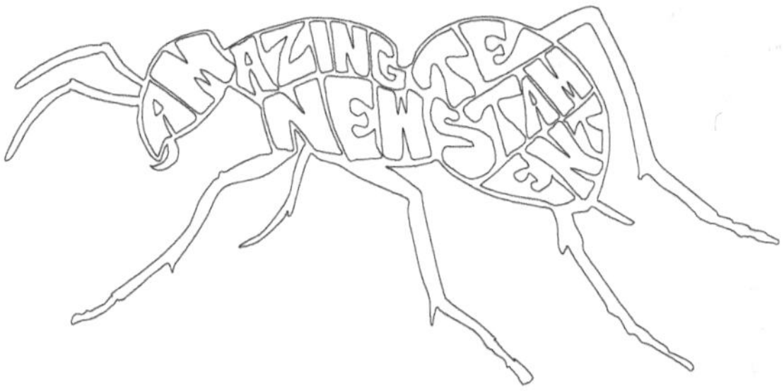

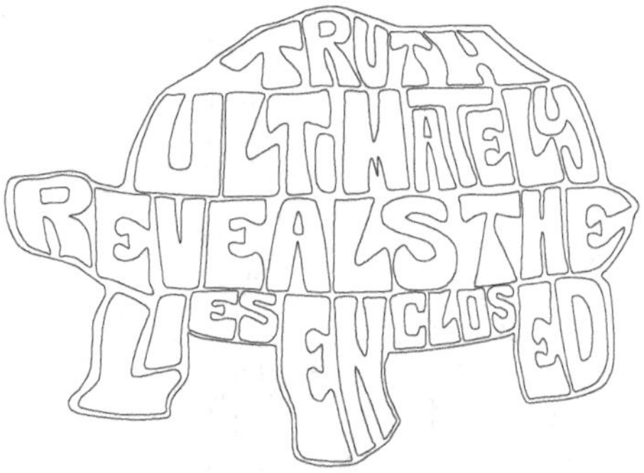

_____

LWO

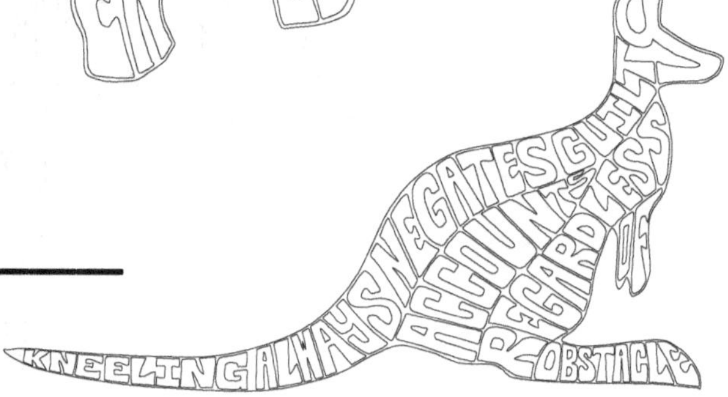

_____

LETRUT _____

TAN

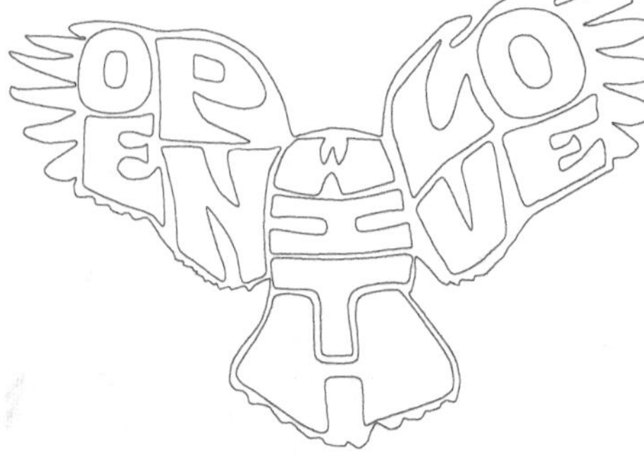

_____

Picture Parable

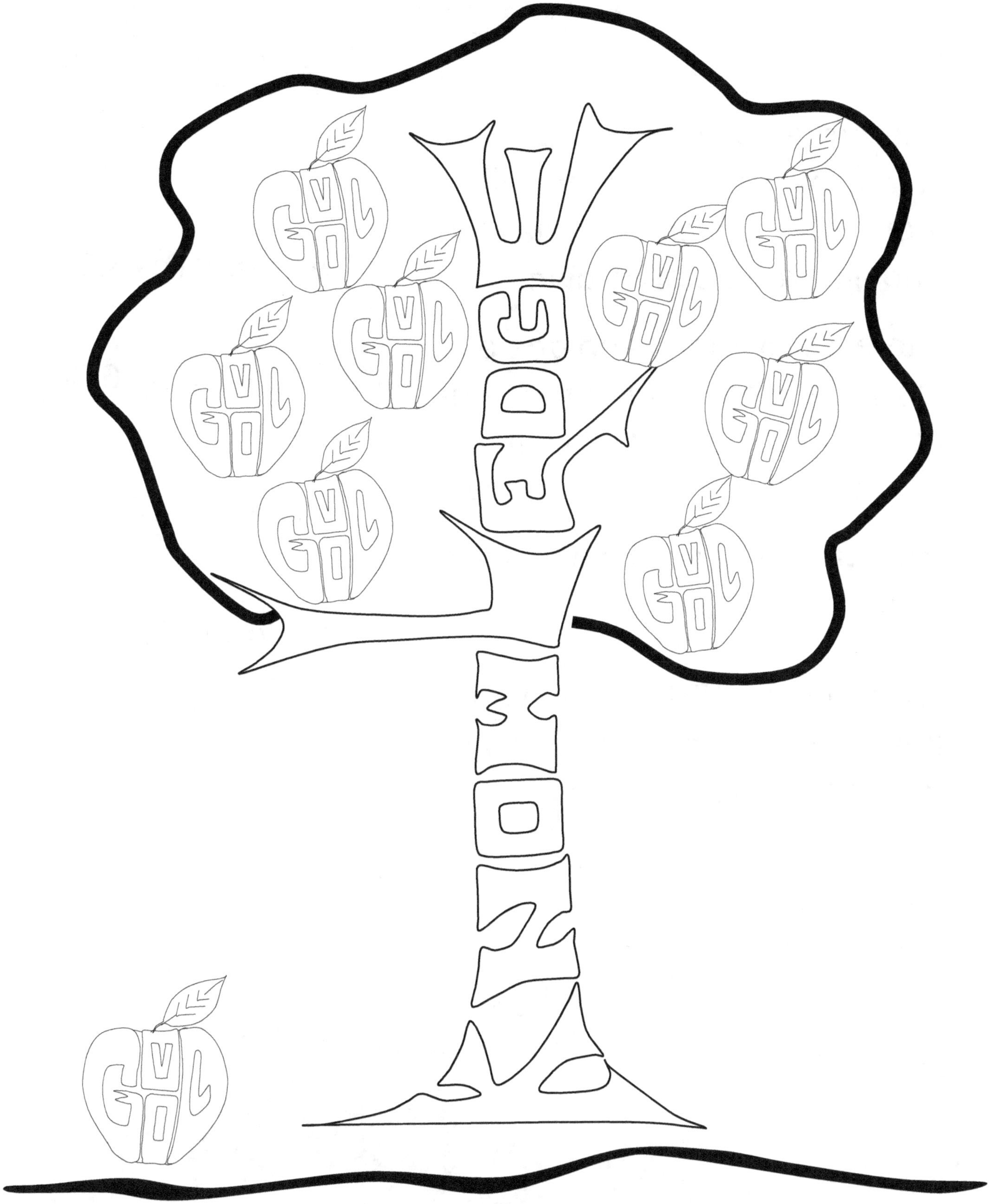

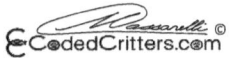

Genesis 3:22

VERSE MATCH
(Draw a line from the verse to the title)

Therefore do not worry about tomorrow, for tomorrow will worry about itself. Each day has enough trouble of its own.

There is salvation in no one else; for there is no other name under heaven that has been given among men by which we must be saved.

Love each other as I have loved you.

Trust in the LORD with all your heart and lean not on your own understanding.

A. Proverbs 3:5

B. Matthew 6:34

C. Acts 4:12

D. John 15:12

ANSWERS

P1. Forever Rely On God
P3. Grace Overcomes Our Sinful Existence
P7. Salvation Happens As Repenters Kneel
P10. TIC TAC TOE
P11. Believers Enjoy Abundant Rewards
P12. All answers are 3
P13. SEAL Deut 4:29, ALLIGATOR Psalms 118:24
   CAT Rev 1:18, SKUNK Isaiah 59:2
P14. CUBES
P15. Honor Our Righteous Savior Eternally
P17. RAM 1 Chron 29:11, LAMB Genesis 2:7
   SWAN Ephesians 6:12, PIG 2 Peter 1:21
P18. B, D, A, C
P19. Trust In God's Eternal Redemption
P23. Believers Ultimately Take The Eternal
   Reward For Loving Yeshua
P25. Remarkable And Majestic
P27. Embracing Almighty God's
   Love Everyday
P29. COLOSSIANS, PHILEMON,
   CORINTHIANS, ROMANS
P31. Christ Almighty Makes Evil Leave
P33. Share The Incredible New Gospel
   Rejoicing All Year
P34. RABBIT, EAGLE, GIRAFFE, BIRD,
   ELEPHANT, APE
P35. Seek Eternal Abiding Love
P36. D, A, C, B
P37. Jesus Arose Giving Us All Redemption
P41. HE AROSE
P42. Lion, Kangaroo, Sheep, Owl, Turtle, Ant
P43. Tree of Knowledge of Good & Evil
P44. B, C, D, A

P 4

P 16

ACROSS
LADYBUG
TURTLE
DOVE
APE
SNAKE

DOWN
LION
BUTTERFLY
GIRAFFE
ELEPHANT
DOLPHIN

P 9

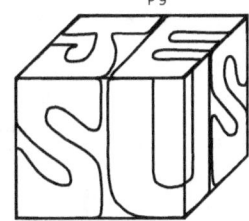

P 21

WE KNOW WHAT REAL LOVE IS BECAUSE
JESUS GAVE US HIS LIFE FIRST. SO
WE ALSO OUGHT TO GIVE UP OUR LIVES
FOR OUR BROTHERS AND SISTERS.

1 John 3:16

P 32

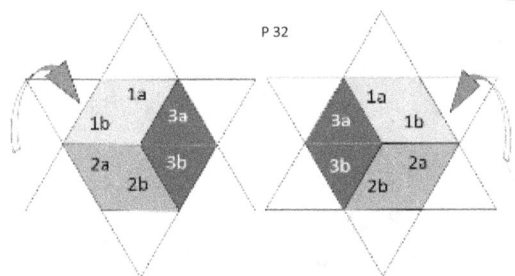

P 6. E (50)

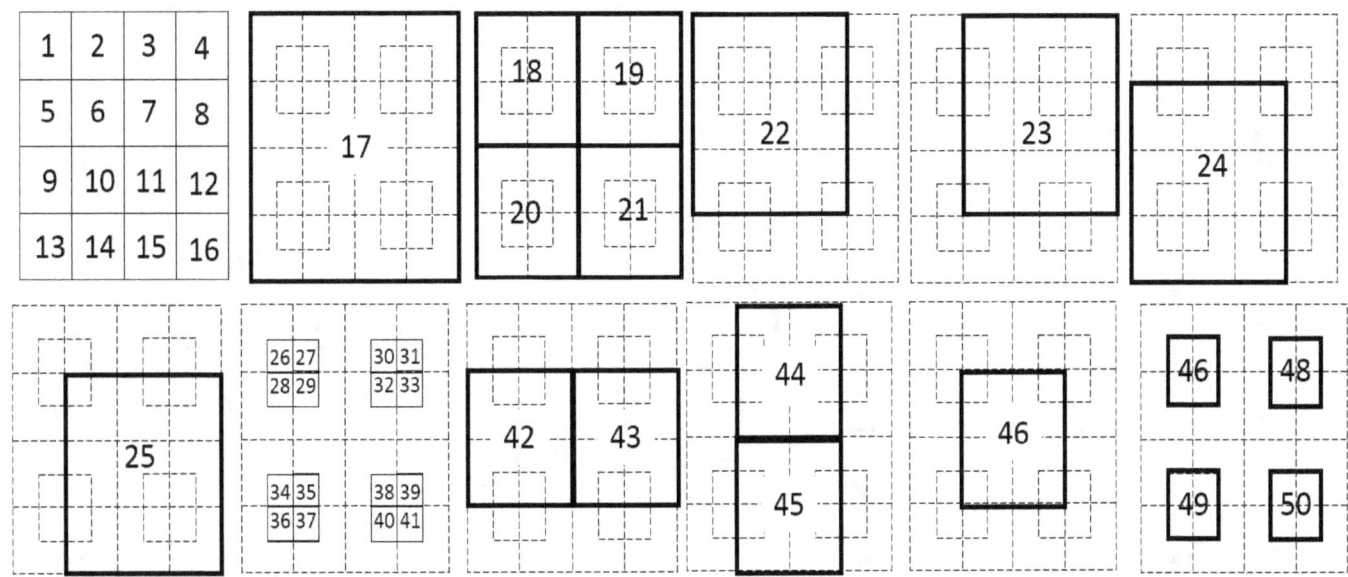

P 5

P 20

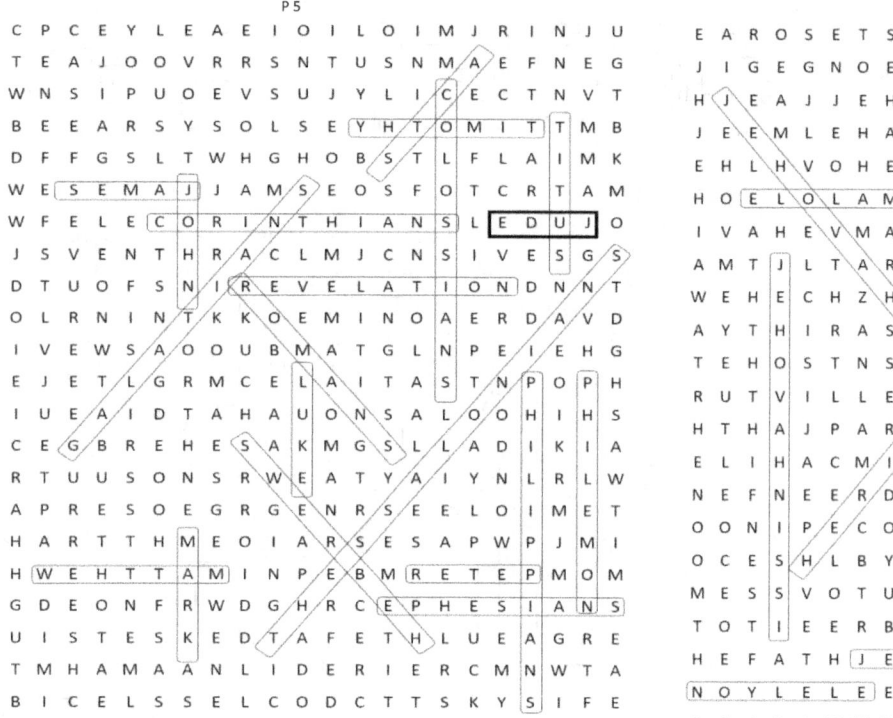

```
C P C E Y L E A E I O I L O I M J R I N J U
T E A J O O V R R S N T U S N M A E F N E G
W N S I P U O E V S U J Y L I C E C T N V T
B E E A R S Y S O L S E Y H T O M I T T M B
D F F G S L T W H G H O B S T L F L A I M K
W E S E M A J J A M S E O S F O T C R T A M
W F E L E C O R I N T H I A N S L E D U J O
J S V E N T H R A C L M J C N S I V E S G S
D T U O F S N I R E V E L A T I O N D N N T
O L R N I N T K K O E M I N O A E R D A V D
I V E W S A O O U B M A T G L N P E I E H G
E J E T L G R M C E L A I T A S T N P O P H
I U E A I D T A H A U O N S A L O O H I H S
C E G B R E H E S A K M G S L L A D I K I A
R T U U S O N S R W E A T Y A I Y N L R L W
A P R E S O E G R G E N R S E E L O I M E T
H A R T T H M E O I A R S E S A P W P J M I
H W E H T T A M I N P E B M R E T E P M O M
G D E O N F R W D G H R C E P H E S I A N S
U I S T E S K E D T A F E T H L U E A G R E
T M H A M A A N L I D E R I E R C M N W T A
B I C E L S S E L C O D C T T S K Y S I F E
```

```
E A R O S E T S I U E L S E L E L J O V M C
J I G E G N O E D G L N J O V J I H A D J E
H J E A J J E H O J A H P A R H A V O H E J
J E E M L E H A V E V Y R N W Z A I A I L S
E H L H V O H E J H O R A D A D J A E J S O
H O E L O L A M E J L R E Z O J E M S U H F
I V A H E V M A N N E S I N E F H T C S A P
A M T J L T A R F I E L A H L E O H H R D A
W E H E C H Z H E R O I O M O N V E S I D E
A Y T H I R A S M J G V J A H I A G T T A C
T E H O S T N S A E A L E C I A H R H A I E
R U T V I L L E M H K M A H M D S E A K E U
H T H A J P A R J E H O H E J D H A A O H S
E L I H A C M I I M A J D D H A A T R M E P
N E F N E E R D E R I E R D S L M I H A E L
O O N I P E C O D C T T S M I E M A A S E S
O C E S H L B Y M E J E H O V S A M V N O O
M E S S V O T U Y A H W E H O H H J O V H R
T O T I E E R B C J A H V O H E J K H T P A
H E F A T H J E H O V A H T S I D K E N U V
N O Y L E L E E V H R N U A N H T N J M O J
B C J D J W W N A E E D E M R E O O J T N U
```

P 28 (E 27 / D72)

Triangle 1: 1 2 3 4 5 6 7 8 9 10 11 12 13 14 15 16 17

18 19 20 21

22

23

24 25 26 27

27 from above

27+6-33

28
29 30
31 32 33

33+3=36

34
35 36

37 38 39 40 41 42
+6 48   +6 54
+6 60   +6 66   +6 72

36+36=72

P 22

Start

Finish

ANSWERS

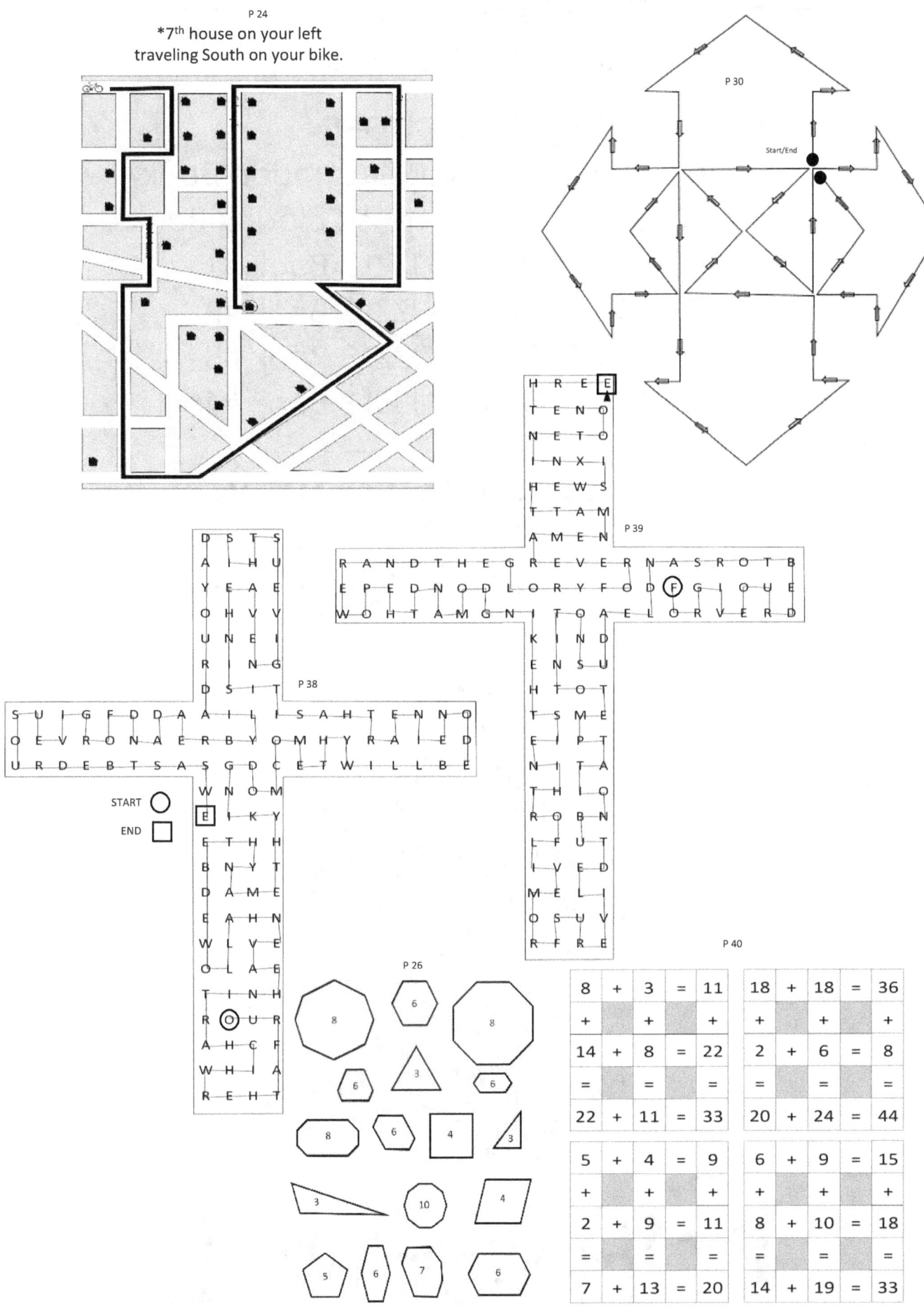

P 24
*7th house on your left
traveling South on your bike.

P 30

P 39

P 38

START ◯
END ☐

P 26

P 40

8	+	3	=	11
+		+		+
14	+	8	=	22
=		=		=
22	+	11	=	33

18	+	18	=	36
+		+		+
2	+	6	=	8
=		=		=
20	+	24	=	44

5	+	4	=	9
+		+		+
2	+	9	=	11
=		=		=
7	+	13	=	20

6	+	9	=	15
+		+		+
8	+	10	=	18
=		=		=
14	+	19	=	33

Other works by:
Michael Massanelli

COLORING BOOKS:
Coded Critters Full Color Illustration Book
Coded Critters All 60 Critters Coloring Book
COD3D COLOR & PUZZL3 Book #1
COD3D COLOR & PUZZL3 Book #2
COD3D COLOR & PUZZL3 Book #3
COD3D COLOR & PUZZL3 Book #4

STRETCHING REVOLUTION
www.StretchingRevolution.com

THE SCIENCE OF EXERCISE
www.MichaelMassanelli.com

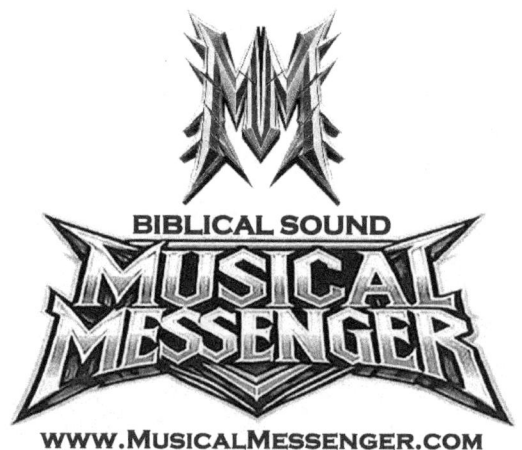

www.MusicalMessenger.com

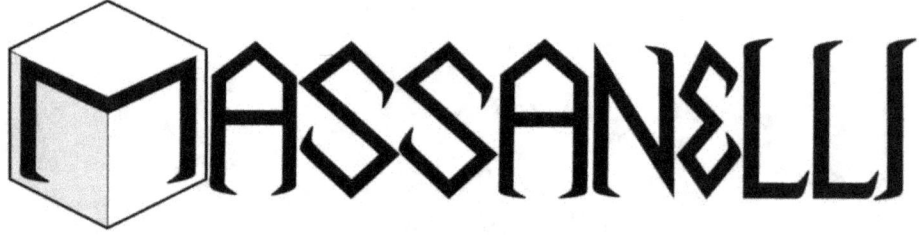